SCIENCE PLUS +

Reactions!

Teacher's Guide

Author **Hans Persson**

UK consultant **Bronwen Howells**

P2 to P3

Years 1-2

Heinemann

Author
Hans Persson

UK consultant
Bronwen Howells

An imprint of Harcourt Education Limited
Heinemann is a registered trademark of Harcourt Education Limited.
© Hans Persson and Liber AB, Stockholm 2006

Acknowledgements
Every effort has been made to contact copyright holders of material reproduced in
this book. Any omissions will be rectified in subsequent printings if notice is given
to the publishers.

10 09 08 07 06
10 9 8 7 6 5 4 3 2 1

ISBN 0 435 01205 3
       9 780435 012052
British Library Cataloguing in Publication Data is available from the British Library
on request.

Published by Harcourt Education, Halley Court, Jordan Hill, Oxford OX2 8EJ
www.myprimary.co.uk
Help and support, plus the widest range of educational solutions

Typeset by **Artistix**
Illustrated by **Matt Buckley** and **Jonathan Edwards**
Cover design by **Tom Cole**
Printed and bound in China by **CTPS**

Welcome to

Reactions!

This book is an attempt to show how you and your class can work with simple, fun science activities to help achieve the objectives set out in the curriculum. The enthusiasm with which children usually carry out practical investigations is bound to make this task all the more rewarding.

Imagine…
You have brought your class to a pond. They are carrying small nets and jars. For many of the children, this is a completely new experience. You can really feel the tension and expectation in the air. There is a lot to investigate!
The children are working in groups; some are rooting around in the weeds while others are turning stones at the edge of the pond. Suddenly, a child comes running up holding a plastic jar. Her eyes are sparkling with the discovery she has made as she shouts and pants for breath: 'Look! You should see this. There are millions of them in the water!' A new world has been revealed.

Introduction

Science is something we all encounter in our everyday lives long before we start school and begin learning about it as a subject. We classify things, mix things, make solutions, and see things melt and solidify. When questions such as 'Why can you see the moon?' or 'Why does a lamp give off light?' arise, we come up with our own explanations. In the natural environment all around us there are key players and countless actors and props which combine to create an ecological drama. We construct our own reasonable explanations for what we see and experience. We accumulate a preliminary understanding of scientific phenomena. Yet our own explanatory models do not always correspond to those constructed by scientists and researchers. It has been shown that we retain these deeply rooted ideas for a very long time.

In order to succeed in the task of reforming children's scientific ideas to accord with accepted or traditional scientific thinking, we need to begin by finding out where the children are in their own thinking. We must sit them down and listen to their explanations. Scientific instruction must give children ample opportunity to formulate their own thoughts verbally, graphically, and in conversation with their classmates. Only when you as a teacher encounter obvious misconceptions in their explanations can you challenge their thinking with questions or investigations that will lead them to reconsider their thinking. Do not wait too long before introducing scientific experiments and ideas. The children's own explanations will continue to burrow away in their minds, and become more difficult to modify as children grow older.

It is easier for a child to learn and evolve explanatory models if he or she is able to experiment, see, feel, hear, taste and smell – and have fun! By making work in the classroom fun, we encourage a positive view of the scientific disciplines in children, their parents and other teachers. 'I feel so popular!' said one teacher participating in a higher education course on chemistry. She had introduced a few scientific experiments in the classroom, and the interest and enjoyment on the part of her pupils was great. These feelings are so contagious that they affect everything the children learn.

Some strategies for organising practical work

There are several familiar classroom settings which lend themselves to practical work in science. You are the best judge of when to use a particular strategy and your decision will be guided by the objectives of the work, the resources available, the experience of the children and any classroom assistants, and whether you have carried out the work before. Here are a few of the key points about some of the most commonly used classroom management strategies.

The whole class working in pairs or groups

In this case, everybody carries out one or more of the same experiments during one working session. This requires more sets of equipment, but is convenient when you want to keep the class together and engage in frequent discussions about the results.

A 'circus' of activities

Here you will need fewer sets of equipment and, if some of the activities involve only the studying of text, you can man a laboratory station to which small groups of children come. In this way you will have the opportunity of listening to the reasoning of individual children.

Modelling to the whole class

There are times when it is appropriate for the teacher to demonstrate either a scientific phenomenon or a scientific method, showing this to the whole class and inviting discussion. If appropriate, the children can go on to ask questions and test their ideas in groups, for example 'What would happen if you did it this way instead?' thereby deepening their understanding. You can also let the children demonstrate for each other, and even for children in other classes. This is an excellent way for them to find out if they really have understood.

Exploring ideas at home

In each chapter there are some activities that are suitable to do at home. They illustrate the same concepts as the classroom activities, but by performing them in a different environment, together with parents or siblings, children's understanding may be deepened. They will see that science is something we encounter every day in the real world. The activities will of course arouse curiosity and new ideas, which will hopefully lead to scientific discussions at home. Bear in mind that Mum and Dad are definitely not expected to have all the answers. These are activities where the child's observations and reflections are the focus.

Following a practical activity at home, each member of the class might draft a report, at his or her own level and according to his or her own abilities, which is taken back to school. You can encourage them to report back in a variety of ways. This is an opportunity for cross-curricular work, especially with literacy (for recounts and reports) and numeracy (for simple data presentation).

Learning to be a scientist

One of the main goals of any science curriculum is to impart a 'deeper understanding of the scientific method', involving the use of scientific enquiry or process-skills. This immediately raises the question: 'How does this method differ from the methods employed in other academic disciplines?' One of the scientific method's particular characteristics is its experimental nature. It is a method for investigating and finding solutions to problems.

Many of the investigations in this book encourage children to think about questions such as 'What do you think will happen if...' or 'How will it change if...' This reflects a very basic premise of the scientific method. You start with a hypothesis, and then test that idea. The word itself, hypothesis, comes from the Greek, and means an educated guess. It has everything to do with prediction, and nothing to do with wild guesses.

The story of science is a story of people with creative minds and bold hypotheses. They had ideas that went against the conventional thinking of their times about how the physical world works. Galileo aimed his telescope into the heavens and voiced thoughts that changed our world view forever. Marie Curie offers another example: after William Roentgen discovered x-rays, Marie set out to find out what caused them. Her fellow scientists were sceptical about her theory that uranium was not the only element to emit radiation. However, she eventually proved that thorium was radioactive, and she also discovered two new radioactive elements, which she called radium and polonium.

Reactions! may not change our picture of the world, but hopefully the pleasure of investigation and problem solving will inspire a generation who might!

Speaking and listening

To stimulate enjoyment and to awaken children's interest, it is very important that we allow them to express themselves at their own level of linguistic sophistication, using the concepts that they have formulated themselves. If they are able to form their own hypotheses and they are personally engaged in scientific investigation, there will arise occasions that challenge their thinking and show them that their assumptions are unreasonable. They will learn at first hand and construct new models of their own that are more in line with accepted theory. This is why it is so important to give children the opportunity to express their thoughts about the investigations, and not merely to conduct them. While working, the children must be given the opportunity to discuss what is going on amongst themselves or with the teacher. These conversations are the junctures at which a lot of knowledge is absorbed. The conversation must be conducted in an open, liberal manner, and all ideas must be respected.

Learning to think scientifically

Both you and your class may need training in how to think scientifically. You can succeed at some things in life by simply following instructions or predetermined paths, but when it comes to science you need to think freely and creatively and have the courage to make bold hypotheses.

Before letting your children loose on the investigations in this book, you can do the following exercise. This will introduce them to the idea of formulating a hypothesis when faced with a science problem. When doing the exercise, ask children to draw and make notes, making sure that they can't see too much of each other's work. You could also let the children think for a while and then present their ideas orally. Give them positive feedback for their efforts. It is important that they produce a variety of suggestions and that you value all of them.

Equipment
- a piece of plastic garden hose about 7 cm long
- a plastic bucket (around 3-litre capacity)
- a plastic lid for the bucket
- a large plastic bottle
- foil
- a plastic bag
- a rubber band
- four jars
- food colouring (two different colours)

Preparing the demonstration

1 Cut a hole the same diameter as the hose in the side of the bucket about a third of the way up. Insert the hose so that it is mostly hanging out of the side of the bucket. You may have to seal around the hole in the bucket with silicone sealant.
2 Cut the top off the plastic bottle to make a funnel.
3 Cover the outside of the funnel with foil.
4 Cut a hole in the bucket lid and insert the funnel.
5 Use the rubber band to attach the plastic bag over the end of the funnel on the underside of the lid.
6 Place a jar next to the bucket and put the end of the hose in it.
7 Fill the bucket with water until a bit runs out of the hose and into the jar. Empty the jar and put it back under the hose.
8 Place the lid on the bucket with the plastic bag hanging inside.
9 Fill the remaining three jars with water. Add one colour to the first, and the other colour to the second. Leave the third colourless.

Performing the demonstration

1 Make sure the bucket is positioned so everyone can see it. Tell the class that you are about to present a mysterious problem!
2 Pour the jar of colourless water into the funnel. The water that comes out of the hose is also colourless.
3 Now pick up one of the jars of coloured water, and pour some into the funnel. The water coming out of the hose is still colourless!
4 Finally, pour the other jar of coloured water into the funnel. Again, the water coming out of the hose is colourless!
5 Make sure that everyone understands what is happening: 'It doesn't matter what colour water I pour in; the water that comes out will always be colourless.'

Give each child a sheet of paper, a pen and two crayons the same colour as the water you used. Ask them to draw a picture of what they think the bucket looks like inside. Through drawing, and words if necessary, they will form a hypothesis. Stress that there are many different possible explanations. What is important right now is what they think. Here are a few examples of what children might suggest:

1 **Two compartments**
Many children suspect that the funnel and bucket are divided in two, and that you pour the coloured water on one side and the colourless water on the other.

2 **Filter**
Suggestions for filters are sand, active charcoal or a coffee filter.

3 **Chemicals**
A common explanation is that some type of chemical may be 'cleaning' the water.

4 **Density**
Many children believe that the fluids have different 'weights', and therefore one 'floats' on the other.

5 **Long hose**
Children may suggest that there is a long hose filled with water in the bucket. The amount of coloured water poured in is not enough to fill the entire hose so it will 'not have time to reach the end'.

6 **Mechanical contraptions**
Sometimes children come up with theories about trapdoors, springs and various contraptions that separate the different fluids.

Many of the children's hypotheses are easy to test. This can be done before you reveal exactly how the bucket is set up.

Classroom safety

Safety guidance can change over time. For up-to-date safety advice, check the CLEAPSS website at www.cleapss.org.uk or consult your LEA guidelines. General science safety advice can be found in *Be Safe!* published by the ASE (ISBN 0 863 57324 X).

The investigations and the equipment in this book have been selected to be as safe as possible. They are drawn primarily from materials typically found at home. However, there are dangerous substances even at home. In kitchens and garages you will find dishwasher liquid, drain cleaner and all kinds of heavy-duty cleaning supplies. These substances are labelled with the same symbols found in chemistry laboratories. This is what the symbols look like:

 Harmful/irritant

 Toxic

 Oxidising

 Explosive

 Flammable

 Dangerous for the environment

 Corrosive

When building up your stock of chemicals, the following rules apply. The chemicals should be labelled with the following information:
- the product's name
- potential risks and a warning symbol
- instructions on how to protect oneself.

Store all chemical securely, locked away in their own cupboard well away from food materials. If you are not sure about where to store a particular substance, check with your science coordinator or headteacher.

Before you begin experimenting, go over these experiment rules with your class.
- Listen to the teacher.
- Read the instructions carefully.
- Do not taste, smell or touch unknown substances.
- Clean up after yourself if you spill.

Read the teacher notes related to the investigation you intend to conduct before you start. A 'Warning!' symbol indicates that you may need to consult safety guidelines.

Chapter	National curriculum	QCA unit	5–14	Northern Ireland	Pages
The human body	Sc1 2b: use first-hand experience and simple information sources to answer questions Sc1 2e: explore, using the sense of sight, hearing, smell, touch and taste as appropriate, and make and record observations and measurements Sc2 2a: to recognise and compare the main external parts of the bodies of humans and other animals Sc2 2c: that taking exercise and eating the right types and amounts of food help humans to keep healthy	1A, 2A, 2C	SIS B: use simple equipment and techniques to make observations and measurements KUL A: name and identify the main external parts of the bodies of humans and other animals	INC a: make observations using their senses KLO a: recognise and name the main external parts of the human body KLO d: develop ideas about how to keep healthy, through exercise, rest, diet, personal hygiene and safety	14–29
Plants	Sc2 3b: to recognise and name the leaf, flower, stem and root of flowering plants Sc2 4b: group living things according to observable similarities and differences Sc2 5a: find out about the different kinds of plants and animals in the local environment Sc2 5b: identify similarities and differences between local environments and ways in which these affect animals and plants that are found there KS2 Sc2 4a: to make and use keys	1B, 2B, 2C	KUL A: sort living things into broad groups according to easily observable characteristics KUL B: identify the main parts of flowering plants KUL C: name some common animals and plants using simple keys	KLA a: find out about the variety of animal and plant life both through direct observations and by using secondary sources KLA c: recognise and name the main parts of a flowering plant including root, stem, leaf and flower KLA d: sort living things into groups using observable features KLA g: observe similarities and differences among animals and among plants	30–43
Animals	Sc1 2a: ask questions and decide how they might find answers to them Sc2 1c: to relate life processes to animals and plants found in the local environment Sc2 4b: group living things according to observable similarities and differences	1A, 2B, 2C	SIS B: make suggestions about what might happen KUL A: sort living things into broad groups according to easily observable characteristics	INP b: talk about what they are going to make and the materials they will use KLA a: find out about the variety of animal and plant life both through direct observations and by using secondary sources KLA d: sort living things into groups using observable features KLA f: find out about some animals, including how they grow, feed, move and use their senses	44–57
Everything can be sorted	Sc1 1: Pupils should be taught that it is important to collect evidence by making observations and measurements when trying to answer a question Sc3 1a: use their senses to explore and recognise the similarities and differences between materials Sc3 1b: sort objects into groups on the basis of simple material properties Sc3 1c: recognise and name common types of material and recognise that some of them are found naturally	1C, 2D	SIS A: make suggestions and contribute to the planning of simple practical explorations KUE A: recognise and name some common materials from living and non-living sources KUE B: make observations of differences in the properties of common materials	INP c: ask questions, discuss ideas and make predictions KMP b: sort a range of everyday objects into groups according to the materials from which they are made KMP c: explore the properties of materials including shape, colour, texture and behaviour	58–77
Solids, liquids and gases	Sc1 2f: explore, using the senses of sight, hearing, smell, touch and taste as appropriate, and make and record observations and measurements Sc3 2b: explore and describe the way some everyday materials change when they are heated or cooled	2D	SIS B: use simple equipment and techniques to make observations and measurements KUE B: describe how everyday materials can be changed by heating or cooling	INC a: make observations using their senses KMC a: find out about the effect of heating and cooling some everyday substances, such as water, chocolate or butter	78–87

Chapter	National curriculum	QCA unit	5–14	Northern Ireland	Pages
Solutions and suspensions	Sc1 2i: compare what happened with what they expected would happen, and try to explain it, drawing on their knowledge and understanding KS2 Sc3 3b: that some solids dissolve in water to give solutions but some do not	1C	KUE B: give examples of everyday materials that dissolve in water	INI d: relate what happened to what they predicted KMC b: investigate which everyday substances dissolve in water	88–99
Magnetism	Sc4 2b: that both pushes and pulls are examples of forces KS2 Sc4 2a: about the forces of attraction and repulsion between magnets, and about the forces of attraction between magnets and magnetic materials	2E	KUF B: describe the interaction of magnets in terms of the forces of attraction and repulsion	KPF a: explore forces which push, pull or make things move	100–111
Air	Sc1 2b: use first-hand experience and simple information sources to answer questions Sc1 2i: compare what happened with what they expected would happen, and try to explain it, drawing on their knowledge and understanding KS2 Sc4 2c: about friction, including air resistance, as a force that slows moving objects and may prevent objects from starting to move	1E, 2E	SIS B: answer questions on the meaning of the findings KUE C: describe air resistance in terms of friction	INI a: talk to the teacher and others about what happened or about what they have made INI d: relate what happened to what they predicted KS2 KPF c: investigate how forces can affect the movement and shape of objects	112–129
Sound	Sc4 3c: that there are many kinds of sound and sources of sound KS2 Sc4 3e: that sounds are made when objects vibrate but that vibrations are not always directly visible	1F	KUF B: link light and sound to seeing and hearing KUF C: link sound to sources of vibration	KPS a: listen to and investigate sources of sounds in their immediate enviroment KPS b: explore ways of making sounds using familiar objects KPS c: investigate how sounds are produced when objects vibrate	130–147
Light	Sc4 3a: to identify different light sources, including the Sun Sc4 3b: that darkness is the absence of light KS2 Sc4 3a: that light travels from a source KS2 Sc4 3c: that light is reflected from surfaces	1D	KUF B: link light and sound to seeing and hearing KUF C: give examples of light being reflected from surfaces	KPL a: find out that light comes from a variety of sources KPL c: explore how light passes through some materials and not others KS2 KPL c: investigate the reflection of light from mirrors and other shiny surfaces	148–165
Electricity	Sc1 2a: ask questions and decide how they might find answers to them Sc4 1a: about everyday appliances that use electricity Sc4 1b: about simple series circuits involving batteries, wires, bulbs and other components Sc4 1c: how a switch can be used to break a circuit	2F	SIS B: use simple equipment and techniques to make observations and measurements KUF A: give examp es of everyday appliances that use electricity KUF C: construct simple battery-operated circuits, identifying the main components	INC a: make observations using their senses KPE a: find out about some uses of electricity in the classroom KS2 KPE b: construct simple circuits using components, such as switches, bulbs and batteries	166–179

What each chapter contains

- A list of the investigations and the learning objectives they aim to meet, plus curriculum links.

- Facts about the topic.

- A story or illustration demonstrating how science is present in everyday life. These stories may be used as an introduction to arouse interest in the subject at hand, or as a way to round off the topic. Either read them out loud or hand out copies for children to see. These stories and illustrations should help children to learn to collect evidence by making observations.

- Notes on the story/illustration. Following each story or illustration is a teacher page containing helpful comments and explanations.

- Classroom investigation pages. Between two and five simple investigations are provided which are designed to successively build on children's understanding and knowledge.

- Accompanying teacher page. Each investigation page is accompanied by teacher notes that consist of: aims and teaching objectives; a summary of the investigation; expected results; an explanation; tips to help the experiment run smoothly; further ideas for investigations or discussion points; and everyday examples of the phenomena in the real world.

- Home investigations.

- Further investigations. Extra ideas for those of you who would like to extend, revise, or follow up a topic.

- A short history of the topic.

Abbreviations used for curriculum strands

National curriculum
Sc1: Scientific Enquiry
Sc2: Life Processes and Living Things
Sc3: Materials and their Properties
Sc4: Physical Processes

5–14
SIS: Skills in science – investigating
KUE: Knowledge and understanding – Earth and space
KUF: Knowledge and understanding – energy and forces
KUL: Knowledge and understanding – living things and the processes of life

Northern Ireland
INC: Investigating and Making – Carrying out and Making
INP: Investigating and Making – Planning
INI: Investigating and Making – Interpreting and Evaluating
KLO: Knowledge and Understanding of Living Things – Ourselves
KLA: Knowledge and Understanding of Living Things – Animals and Plants
KMP: Knowledge and Understanding of Materials – Properties
KMC: Knowledge and Understanding of Materials – Change
KME: Knowledge and Understanding of Materials – Environment
KPF: Knowledge and Understanding of Physical Processes – Forces and Energy
KPE: Knowledge and Understanding of Physical Processes – Electricity
KPS: Knowledge and Understanding of Physical Processes – Sound
KPL: Knowledge and Understanding of Physical Processes – Light

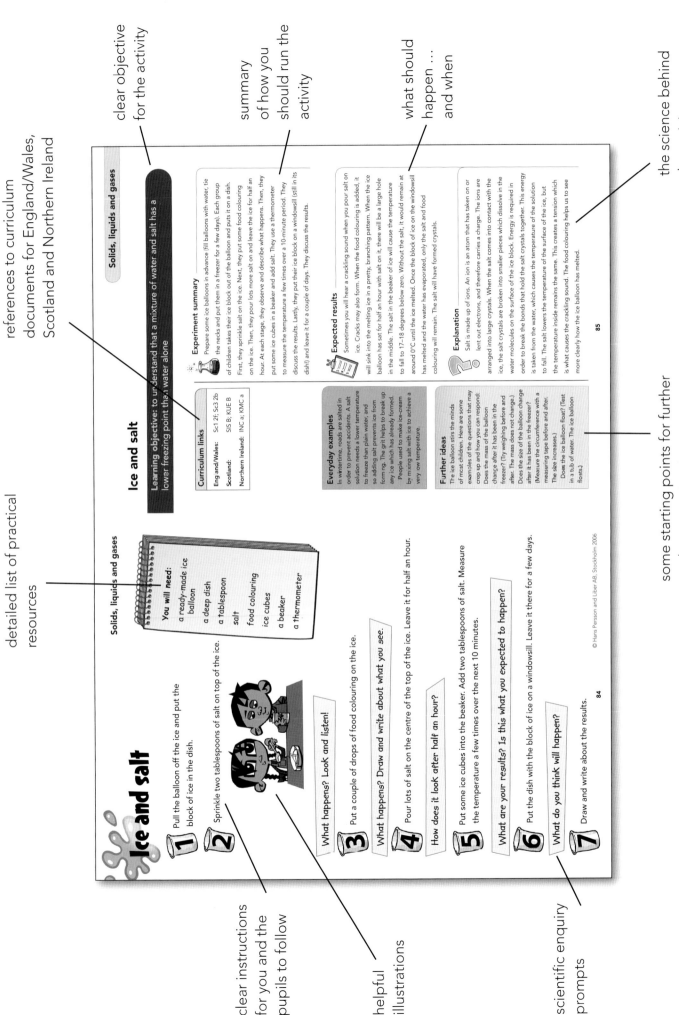

references to curriculum documents for England/Wales, Scotland and Northern Ireland

clear objective for the activity

summary of how you should run the activity

what should happen … and when

the science behind the activity

detailed list of practical resources

helpful illustrations

clear instructions for you and the pupils to follow

scientific enquiry prompts

some starting points for further work or investigation

Solids, liquids and gases

Ice and salt

Learning objective: to understand that a mixture of water and salt has a lower freezing point than water alone

Curriculum links

Eng and/Wales:	Sc1 2f; Sc3 2b
Scotland:	SIS B; KUE B
Northern Ireland:	INC a; KMC a

Experiment summary

Prepare some ice balloons in advance (fill balloons with water, tie the necks and put them in a freezer for a few days). Each group of children takes their ice block out of the balloon and puts it on a dish. First, they sprinkle salt on the ice. Next, they put some food colouring on the ice. Then, they pour lots more salt on and leave the ice for half an hour. At each stage, they observe and describe what happens. Then, they put some ice cubes in a beaker and add salt. They use a thermometer to measure the temperature a few times over a 10-minute period. They discuss the results. Lastly, they put their ice block on a windowsill (still in its dish) and leave it for a couple of days. They discuss the results.

Expected results

Sometimes you will hear a crackling sound when you pour salt on ice. Cracks may also form. When the food colouring is added, it will sink into the melting ice in a pretty, branching pattern. When the ice balloon has sat for half an hour with salt on it, there will be a large hole in the middle. The salt in the beaker of ice will cause the temperature to fall to 17–18 degrees below zero. Without the salt, it would remain at around 0°C until the ice melted. Once the block of ice on the windowsill has melted and the water has evaporated, only the salt and food colouring will remain. The salt will have formed crystals.

Explanation

Salt is made up of ions. An ion is an atom that has taken on or lent out electrons, and therefore carries a charge. The ions are arranged into large crystals. When the salt comes into contact with the ice, the salt crystals are broken into smaller pieces which dissolve in the water molecules on the surface of the ice block. Energy is required in order to break the bonds that hold the salt crystals together. This energy is taken from the water, which causes the temperature of the solution to fall. The salt lowers the temperature of the surface of the ice, but the temperature inside remains the same. This creates a tension which is what causes the crackling sound. The food colouring helps us to see more clearly how the ice balloon has melted.

85

Solids, liquids and gases

Ice and salt

You will need:

- a ready-made ice balloon
- a deep dish
- a tablespoon
- salt
- food colouring
- ice cubes
- a beaker
- a thermometer

1 Pull the balloon off the ice and put the block of ice in the dish.

2 Sprinkle two tablespoons of salt on top of the ice.

What happens? Look and listen!

3 Put a couple of drops of food colouring on the ice.

What happens? Draw and write about what you see.

4 Pour lots of salt on the centre of the top of the ice. Leave it for half an hour.

How does it look after half an hour?

5 Put some ice cubes into the beaker. Add two tablespoons of salt. Measure the temperature a few times over the next 10 minutes.

What are your results? Is this what you expected to happen?

6 Put the dish with the block of ice on a windowsill. Leave it there for a few days.

What do you think will happen?

7 Draw and write about the results.

Everyday examples

In wintertime, roads are salted in order to prevent accidents. A salt solution needs a lower temperature to freeze than plain water, and so adding salt prevents ice from forming. The grit helps to break up any ice which has already formed.
People used to make ice-cream by mixing salt with ice to achieve a very ow temperature.

Further ideas

The ice balloon stirs the minds of most children. Here are some examples of the questions that may crop up and how you can respond: Does the mass of the balloon change after it has been in the freezer? (try weighing before and after. The mass does not change.) Does the size of the balloon change after it has been in the freezer? (Measure the circumference with a measuring tape before and after. The size increases.)
Does the ice balloon float? (Test in a tub of water. The ice balloon floats.)

84

13

The human body

Investigation	Curriculum links

Classroom investigations

How is it moving?

to associate images of a skeleton with the bones in your own body

Sc1 2b: use first-hand experience and simple information sources to answer questions

Sc2 2a: to recognise and compare the main external parts of the bodies of humans and other animals

KUL A: name and identify the main external parts of the bodies of humans and other animals

KLO a: recognise and name the main external parts of the human body

One big breath

to find out how much air fits in the lungs

Sc1 2e: explore, using the sense of sight, hearing, smell, touch and taste as appropriate, and make and record observations and measurements

SIS B: use simple equipment and techniques to make observations and measurements

INC a: make observations using their senses

Heart rates

to observe how the pulse changes when working and at rest

Sc2 2c: that taking exercise and eating the right types and amounts of food help humans to keep healthy

KUL A: describe some ways in which humans keep themselves safe

KLO d: develop ideas about how to keep healthy, through exercise, rest, diet, personal hygiene and safety

How far can you run on a dream sandwich?

to understand that food gives us energy

Sc2 2c: that taking exercise and eating the right types and amounts of food help humans to keep healthy

KUL A: describe some ways in which humans keep themselves safe

KLO d: develop ideas about how to keep healthy, through exercise, rest, diet, personal hygiene and safety

Home investigations

Fingerprints

Further investigations

X-ray picture

Facts about...
the human body

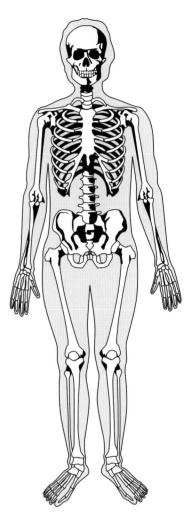

Putting it all together

The body is made up of various systems and organs: lungs that take care of breathing, blood that transports nutrients and muscles that allow us to move. All of these are systems with specialised tasks which, when put together, make up a greater whole.

Skeleton

The skeleton provides stability and protection, and manufactures red blood cells.

Muscles

Muscles hold the skeleton together and allow us to move.

Respiratory system

The lungs supply the blood with oxygen, which is used by every cell in the body. The lungs also expel carbon dioxide as waste.

Digestive system

The stomach and intestines break food down into small pieces that enter into the blood stream. The blood then carries the nutrients from the food to all the cells of the body.

Circulatory system

The bloodstream transports oxygen, nutrients and waste. Blood also contains the body's internal defences against illness. Hormones are also transported in the bloodstream.

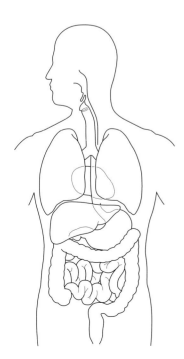

Organs and cells

Our organs are made up of tiny cells. They are so small that they are hard to study, even under a microscope. Cells may not all look alike, but they are all made up of the same parts.

Nervous system

The nervous system regulates the rest of the body's systems. Sensory organs sense what is in our environment and report changes to the brain.

A HARD STORY TO STOMACH

Jamie is reading a science magazine.

Notes on the story

Fact or fiction?

It's actually true! On June 6 1822, the 18-year-old Canadian youth Alex St. Martin was shot accidentally in the stomach. William Beaumont, an army doctor who examined the wound 30 minutes after the bullet was fired, made a detailed report of this. He had no idea that this patient would lead to many years of successful research and would make both Alex and the doctor himself famous.

The unusual wound

In the beginning, food would not remain long in Alex's stomach, and would come trickling out of the hole. Things improved once Beaumont had applied a better bandage to the stomach wound. The strange thing that happened next was that despite the doctor's best efforts to get the hole in Alex's stomach to heal, it just wouldn't. Instead, a layer of skin that resembled a lid or door grew over the hole – and it was possible to open this door!

The door in Alex's stomach

Beaumont realised that he would now be able to study how food is digested and how the stomach works, using a living patient. All he had to do was open the door, so to speak. He performed many successful experiments this way. Many important discoveries about the way we digest food came out of these investigations.

The digestive system

In the past, it was thought that the stomach was like a kettle in which food was boiled down. Beaumont conducted experiments by tying small pieces of different foods along a piece of thread, feeding it into the hole in Alex's stomach, and pulling it out later to observe what had happened to each type of food. Through these experiments he was able to show that stomach acids broke the food down chemically.

Science fiction?

Meena thinks the story is made up. A certain scepticism towards the astounding stories that can be read in science magazines is understandable, and this can form a good talking point and cross-curricular link to Literacy.

How is it moving?

 Look at the three pictures below.

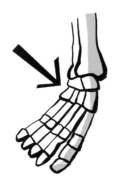 

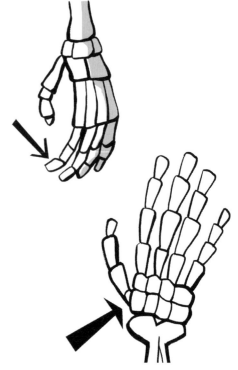

 Move the parts of your body that the arrows are pointing to.

 Look at the picture of the hand.

 By moving only the joint that the arrow is pointing to, try to pick up your pen!

 Now write your name! Try using both hands – one at a time!

 Look at the picture of the skeleton.

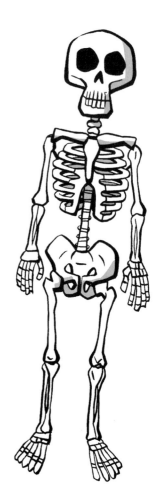

 Point to joints on the skeleton and ask a friend to move the part of their body that you are pointing at.

Show the others in your class.

How is it moving?

Learning objective: to associate images of a skeleton with the bones in your own body

Curriculum links

England/Wales:	Sc1 2b; Sc2 2a
Scotland:	KUL A
Northern Ireland:	KLO a

Further ideas

Ask the children to come up with questions about skeletons and bones. Why do we have a skeleton? How many bones are there in the human body? (about 200) Which bone is the largest? (the femur) Which are the smallest? (the bones in the ear) Why do we have ribs? (They protect the internal organs while still making it possible to breathe.) How do we grow if bones are so hard? (they are softer in newborns) Why does a skull look the way it does? (to accommodate holes for the nose and eyes)

In order for bones in the body to be able to move, they are connected to one another by different kinds of joints. There are ball joints and hinge joints. Where are these different types of joints found in the body? Feel around and think about it to find out! Ligaments are what hold bones in place.

Investigation summary

Children look at pictures of parts of a skeleton and move the joints that are indicated by arrows. They try to pick up a pen and write their name using only their thumb joint. They point to joints on a picture of a skeleton and ask a classmate to move the matching parts of their body.

Expected results

Children should move their ankles (by lifting the front of their foot off the ground or by rotating their ankle), jaws (by moving their bottom jaw from side to side) and finger joints (by wiggling the tip of their index finger) as indicated by the first three pictures. They will probably find it very tricky to pick up the pen and write their names using only their thumb joint, but it is possible with a little patience!

Explanation

The skeleton serves many different functions. It gives support and rigidity, it protects parts of the body – for example the brain and spinal cord – and it manufactures red blood cells. The bones contain something called bone marrow. This marrow is what generates red blood cells.

One big breath

You will need:

a bucket

a high-sided tray

water

a large, plastic food bag with no holes

a wire bag tie

a ruler

a 1-litre measure

 1 Stand the bucket in the tray then fill the bucket right up to the brim with water.

 2 Flatten the bag so that it does not contain any air.

 3 Scrunch the top of the bag together to allow you to blow into it as if it were a balloon.

 4 Take a deep breath and blow the entire breath into the bag.

 5 Twist a bag tie around the top of the bag to stop the air escaping.

 6 Put the bag on the surface of the water in the bucket.

 7 Carefully push it down using the tip of a ruler until the bag is completely under the surface. Your hand is not allowed to enter the water!

 8 Carefully lift the bucket out of the tray. Make sure you don't spill any more water into the tray!

 9 Pour the water from the tray into the 1-litre measure.

 10 Record how much water is in the measure.

 11 Compare your results with your friends'.

Can you work out how much air you and your friends had in your lungs?

20

One big breath

Learning objective: to find out how much air fits in the lungs

Curriculum links

England/Wales:	Sc1 2e
Scotland:	SIS B
Northern Ireland:	INC a

It is best if each child blows into their bag separately, so that you can supervise each of them. If children suffer from asthma, we do not recommend that they take part in this activity.

Investigation summary

Children find out how much air they can breathe into their lungs by blowing one big breath into a plastic bag (these need to be large, with no holes – food bags are best). They measure the volume of air in the bag by pushing it under the surface of a bucket of water filled to the brim, and measuring how much water overflows.

Tips

The challenge of relating the water displaced to the measurement of air in the lungs is complex for many in this age group. They will need careful explanation of what has happened. A good problem-solving exercise is to let children try to sort out how to measure the volume of air in the bag themselves.

There are lung capacity devices available for purchase known as spirometers which make the activity easier to grasp, although they can be expensive. The simplest kind is made from a type of graduated plastic bag.

Expected results

The usual lung capacity for a 6- or 7-year-old is between 2 and 4 litres. Adults can breathe up to 6 litres of air into their lungs. Even though it feels as if you are blowing out all the air from your lungs, there is still about a litre left!

Explanation

A common misconception held by children and even adults is that the lungs are like a bag or balloon inside the body. Actually, the lungs bear a greater resemblance to a sponge. The windpipe, or trachea, leads from the throat to the lungs, where it branches out into smaller and smaller pipes. The smallest of these pipes have alveoli attached to them. There are 300 million alveoli in the lungs, and if it were possible to open all the alveoli and flatten them out, they would cover an area equal to half a tennis court (100 m²). Every tiny alveolus is wrapped in and surrounded by thin, blood-bearing capillaries. The blood takes oxygen from the alveoli and releases carbon dioxide. All the body's cells need oxygen for combustion (to live) and the by-product that occurs in combustion is carbon dioxide. When we breathe out, we get rid of this carbon dioxide, which the body does not need.

Further ideas

Ask the children to investigate how much air they expel in a normal breath.

Heart rates

 Take your friend's pulse. Place two fingers on their wrist and count the number of beats.

 **You will need:** a watch with a second hand

How many times does your friend's heart beat in 1 minute?

 Now ask your friend to take your pulse.

How many times does your heart beat in 1 minute?

 Record the results for both of you.

 Run a lap around the school or run on the spot for 5 minutes.

 Take each other's pulse again, and record the results.

 Sit or lie down and rest for 3 minutes.

 Take each other's pulse again, and record the results.

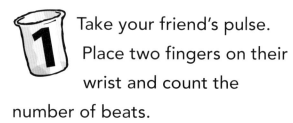 Present your results in a simple table.

Did your heart rates change? Why do you think this is?

Heart rates

Learning objective: to observe how the pulse changes when working and at rest

Curriculum links

England/Wales:	Sc2 2c
Scotland:	KUL A
Northern Ireland:	KLO d

 Be aware that the physical exercise suggested may not be appropriate for children with conditions such as asthma.

Further ideas

You can use a stethoscope to listen carefully to the heartbeat. Look for different places to take your pulse. What does the chest sound like? How about the forehead?

Investigation summary

Children work in either pairs or groups and take each other's pulse by placing two fingers lightly on the other person's wrist and counting the number of beats in 1 minute. (Alternatively, children could count the number of beats in 10 or 15 seconds, then multiply by 6 or 4 to find the number of beats per minute.) Children then do some physical exercise for 5 minutes, take their pulses again, then rest for 3 minutes, and take their pulses again. Each child then records all the results for themselves and the others in their group in a simple table. Alternatively, they could come up with their own way of presenting their results.

Tips

A good ICT link would be to use a pulse-meter.

Expected results

The average resting heart rate for 6- or 7-year-olds is around 90 beats per minute. Adults usually have a lower heart rate, usually around 70 beats per minute. When the cardiovascular system is placed under strain, the pulse rises. After resting for a while, the heart rate returns to normal. The heart rate of a person who is in good shape will return to normal faster than that of someone who is unfit.

Explanation

The entire body is made up of small cells. Every cell in the body needs oxygen, fuel and construction material for us to remain alive. Blood is responsible for transporting these substances. The heart is a hollow muscle that pumps blood through vessels of differing width. Every time the heart contracts to pump blood, a pulse is generated. When at work, the muscles need more oxygen and nutrients, causing the heart to beat faster (up to 200 beats per minute). At 200 beats per minute, 20 to 30 litres of blood will pass through the heart's chambers per minute. The resting volume is only 5 litres per minute. The total volume of blood in an adult body is around 5 litres.

How far can you run on a dream sandwich?

We eat because our bodies need construction material and vitamins, and because we need energy to be able to do everything we need to. Food is our fuel. We can calculate the amount of energy in each piece of food that we eat.

You will need:

charts (your teacher will hand these out later)

Which foods in the grid below would you put in your dream sandwich? You cannot use more than 100 grams of food!

 Colour all the foods that you want to put in your sandwich.

ham, 40 g	cucumber, 10 g	tuna, 40 g	chicken, 50 g
egg, 20 g	pickle, 10 g	tomato, 10 g	cheese, 20 g
coleslaw, 10 g	salmon, 30 g	sausage, 40 g	lettuce, 10 g

How much energy do you think your dream sandwich would give you? How many metres do you think you could run on this energy?

 Now ask your teacher for the chart telling you how much energy your fillings will give you.

 Work out the total number of kilocalories your sandwich will give you.

 Work out the total number of metres you could run on this energy.

How far can you run on a dream sandwich?

Learning objective: to understand that food gives us energy

Curriculum links

England/Wales:	Sc2 2c
Scotland:	KUL A
Northern Ireland:	KLO d

Investigation summary

Copy the chart below and make enough copies for each child/group of children to have one each. Children choose foods from the grid of 12 items and colour the ones they would put in their dream sandwich. They cannot use more than 100 grams of food. Explain that the sandwich is made using whatever bread they like best, with margarine or butter, and this does not count towards their 100 grams, or their energy total. Hand out the charts. Children work out how many kilocalories of energy are in their sandwich, and how far it would allow them to run.

The chart is based on a variety of sources claiming that 10 kilocalories per minute are needed to run 7 km/h. Please note that the conversion of kilocalories to metres of running is drastically oversimplified!

Tips

You may want to use this opportunity to discuss what makes food healthy, what is tasty, and what should not be eaten to avoid illness.

Food	Weight	Kilocalories	Metres of running
ham	40 g	100 kcal	1200 m
cucumber	10 g	1 kcal	12 m
tuna	40 g	75 kcal	900 m
chicken	50 g	75 kcal	900 m
egg	20 g	30 kcal	360 m
pickle	10 g	12 kcal	144 m
tomato	10 g	2 kcal	24 m
cheese	20 g	80 kcal	960 m
coleslaw	10 g	15 kcal	180 m
salmon	30 g	35 kcal	420 m
sausage	40 g	112 kcal	1344 m
lettuce	10 g	1 kcal	12 m

Explanation

The body needs balanced nutrition. This is especially important during the growing years. If the body lacks any of the substances it needs, it grows ill. Symptoms of malnutrition arise (for example anaemia). Food is usually divided into three main groups: carbohydrate, protein and fat. Carbohydrate and fat are used as fuel. Protein is used by the body as building blocks, among other things. Vitamins and minerals are other important substances found in food.

Home investigation

Fingerprints

 Wet your thumb with a bit of water.

 Paint your thumb with watercolour paint.

 Press your thumb on the centre of the first box below, and roll it a little from side to side.

You will need:
water
watercolour paint
paintbrush

4 Ask five other people to make their thumb prints in the other boxes.

 Take the prints to school and look at them very closely.

What different shapes can you see in the thumb prints?

Home investigation teacher notes

Fingerprints

Investigation summary

Children collect six thumb prints, including their own. They paint the thumbs with watercolour paint, and then press them onto their worksheet to make a print. Children bring their six thumb prints into school, where they look at them very carefully, using a magnifying glass or microscope if your school has one. They look for different shapes in the prints.

Expected results

Everyone's skin has a unique pattern. No two sets of fingerprints are identical. These are the three main shapes that children may be able to see:

whorl   arch   coil

Further ideas

Do all your fingers have the same pattern? Are the left and right thumbs identical? Make five fingerprints on a sheet of paper, with two from the same finger. Can the children find the double?

Further investigations

X-ray picture

Investigation

Photocopy this X-ray picture onto an OHP transparency. Show the 'X-ray' to the children, and ask them to think about what might have happened to the arm in the picture.

Explanation

The bone was broken, but pins were used to hold it in place, and it has now healed.

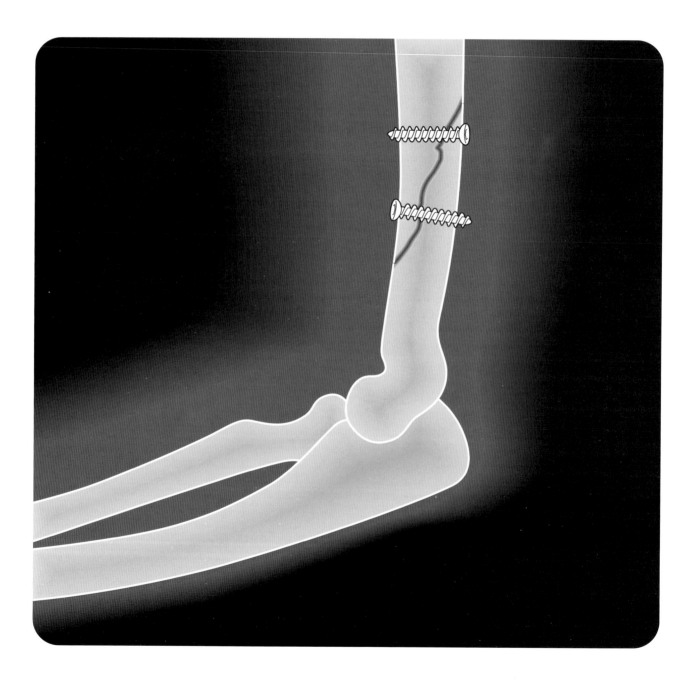

A short history of...
the human body

Doctor or medicine man?

It has always been important for humans to know a thing or two about how the body works, particularly for being able to treat and cure illnesses. People performed standardised operations as early as the Stone Age, as did the ancient Egyptians, who practised advanced medicine in 1500 BC. The Greek philosopher Hippocrates (460–377 BC) advocated a procedure that is a matter of course to us now. Instead of messing around with exorcism, amulets and other forms of ignorant 'magic', he told doctors to listen carefully to their patients and be thorough.

Leonardo da Vinci

The Italian artist Leonardo da Vinci (1452–1511) is famous for his many talents. He is often referred to as a universal genius. By da Vinci's time, there were a few places in Italy where it was permitted to dissect human bodies. His anatomical drawings of organs, muscles and ligaments represented a great advance for biology. He was the first to study the uterus, and he made pioneering discoveries about the structure of the heart and circulatory system.

Dissection forbidden

Another man who advocated thorough study of the body and all its parts, instead of reliance on magic, was the Italian physician Claudius Galenus (130–200). He wanted to cut open (dissect) human bodies to discover how they worked, but this was banned in Rome. He later reasoned that there must be many similarities between the insides of humans and animals. His discoveries were long thought to be completely credible, and the 'anatomy' he described in a series of books continued to exert great influence over medical minds for many years.

Body snatching

Those who know the story of Dr Frankenstein and his project know that the story in part has to do with stealing newly dead corpses and their body parts. This is reminiscent of the methods of the Flemish physician Andreas Vesalius (1514–1564). His toying with brains and guts eventually led to ground-breaking anatomical discoveries, and his books are the basis of modern anatomy.

The mapping of the circulatory system

When Galenus described the circulatory system, he said that blood was propelled through the body in waves. This theory lasted for many centuries. The Englishman William Harvey (1578–1657) claimed that blood is in constant circulation instead. He found valves in the bloodstream that gave credit to this theory. The results he presented were greeted with the utmost scepticism by his peers. Despite the fact that they were based on careful experiments and investigations, it took some 50 years for his bold ideas to be taken seriously.

Investigation	Curriculum links

Classroom investigations

Sorting plants
to sort and classify various plants

Sc2 4b: group living things according to observable similarities and differences
KUL A: sort living things into broad groups according to easily observable characteristics
KLA d: sort living things into groups using observable features

Comparing plants
to observe and describe similarities and differences between two plants

Sc2 3b: to recognise and name the leaf, flower, stem and root of flowering plants
KUL B: identify the main parts of flowering plants
KLA c: recognise and name the main parts of a flowering plant including root, stem, leaf and flower

Collecting plants
to learn to recognise some common plants in the local environment

Sc2 5a: find out about the different kinds of plants and animals in the local environment
Sc2 5b: identify similarities and differences between local environments and ways in which these affect animals and plants that are found there
KUL A: recognise and name some common plants and animals found in the local environment
KLA a: find out about the variety of animal and plant life both through direct observations and by using secondary sources

Identifying plants
to use a classification key to help identify plants

Sc2 4b: group living things according to observable similarities and differences
KS2 Sc2 4a: to make and use keys
KUL C: name some common animals and plants using simple keys
KLA d: sort living things into groups using observable features
KLA g: observe similarities and differences among animals and among plants

Further investigations

Playing with plants

Dandelions

Water plants

Facts about...
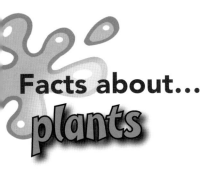
plants

The plant kingdom

At present, around 300 000 plant species are known around the world. This gigantic plant kingdom contains amazing variety and divergences, from the tiniest, most microscopic algae to the huge redwood tree. There are plants adapted to life in extreme heat and cold, plants whose seeds can survive forest fires, and flowers that can be smelt from several kilometres away.

Linnaeus's system

The basis of plant classification was established by the Swedish naturalist Carolus Linnaeus in the 1700s. In brief, the system for classifying plants originated by Linnaeus is based on counting the sexual organs in flowers and then arranging them into different families based on the number counted. To find a simple system for naming all living organisms, that could be used with ease around the world, he assigned Latin names to all the plants he gathered. First comes the name of the genus, then the name of the species.

Classifying plants

Botanists sort plants into groups according to characteristics of stems, roots, leaves, flowers and fruit. This method of sorting is known as classification. The plant kingdom can be arranged into groups in a variety of ways, and there are several different systems used across the world. One simple way of classifying plants is by arranging them into the following four groups:
Bryophytes (mosses and liverworts)
Pteridophytes (ferns, horsetails and club mosses)
Gymnosperms (conifers, yews, cycads and ginkgos)
Angiosperms (flowering plants)
Originally, our 'plant kingdom' included bacteria, diatoms, dinoflagellates, fungi, and slime moulds, but these are no longer categorised as plants.

The life cycle of a plant

Flowers have male and female parts. The male parts produce pollen, and the female parts produce eggs (ovules). To produce seeds, the pollen has to reach the ovules. This process is called pollination, and it can be carried out by insects such as bees, or by the wind. When the pollen and the ovule fuse together, a seed is formed. This is called fertilisation. The plant then needs to spread its seeds around in order to create new plants. There are four ways in which seeds can be dispersed: animals eat the fruit and the seeds get dropped afterwards; some seeds are in pods which 'explode'; some light seeds are blown by the wind; and some seeds are carried away by water.

WHO WAS LINNAEUS?

This is Carolus Linnaeus. He lived from 1707-1778.

The three smaller pictures show the male and female parts in detail, as well as what is inside a seed.

These two plants are actually the same species. Linnaeus discovered that plants have male and female parts. The plant in the picture is a bit unusual. One of the plants has male flowers, and the other has female flowers.

On the back is a bee drawing nectar from a flower. Grains of pollen can be seen on the flower's stamen. Pollen has stuck to the bee's leg. The insect fertilises flowers by moving pollen from the stamen of one plant to the pistil of another.

Notes on the story

The 100 kronor note

This Swedish banknote portrays one of Sweden's greatest men of science, Carolus Linnaeus. To the right of his portrait is the year 1729 and some text from his groundbreaking treatise *Praeludia Sponsalorium Plantarum*. You can read more about Linnaeus on pages 31 and 43.

Male and female parts of flowers

Inside flowers, Linnaeus found a stamen (the male sexual organ) and a pistil (the female organ), which contains the stigma and nectar. The result of the sexual fertilisation is a seed. This is the flower's offspring. Inside the seed, there is both a baby plant and food. Some plants, such as the one on the banknote (dog's mercury), have individual plants that are either male or female, rather than having flowers with both male and female parts. Some plants, such as stinging nettles, have individual male and female flowers on the same plant.

Pollination

Pollination means the transfer of pollen from the male to the female part of the flower. This usually happens when insects get pollen on their feet and transfer it to another flower, or when the wind blows the pollen from one flower to another. When a grain of pollen reaches the stigma (which is inside the pistil), a tiny pollen tube extends down into the ovary and into the egg. Then sperm cells travel down the pollen tube, and fertilise the egg. This fertilisation process is what creates seeds, which go on to grow into new plants.

Sorting plants

 Cut out the pictures of the plants.

 Sort the plants into groups that you think make sense.

You will need:

scissors

glue

A3 paper

 Stick the groups onto a large piece of paper.

 Label each group with the name or word you think best describes it.

birch	oak	tulip	grass
water lily	buttercup	rose	bulrush
bluebell	spruce	pine	daisy
strawberry	dandelion	carrot	nettle

Sorting plants

Learning objective: to sort and classify various plants

Curriculum links

England/Wales:	Sc2 4b
Scotland:	KUL A
Northern Ireland:	KLA d

Investigation summary

Children cut out the 16 pictures of plants and sort them into sets that they think are appropriate. They then make displays of their sets on large sheets of paper, labelling each set with a suitable name or word. This activity works well in small groups, as it gives the children a chance to discuss various classification options. Emphasise that there are a number of ways to classify. It's not a matter of arriving at the 'correct' answer. A slightly different way of doing it would be to ask each group to stick their pictures onto their large sheet of paper, but not to label the sets. Each group can then present their ideas to the rest of the class, with the other children asking questions about how they classified the plants.

Tips

It is a good idea to enlarge the pictures using a photocopier.

Expected results

The children will come up with different ideas about how to sort the plants. They might come up with sets such as 'Flowers you can plant', 'Edible plants', 'Water plants', 'Weeds', 'Trees', and so on. The point is to get an idea of how much the children understand by letting them have fun. After looking at all their suggestions, you could look together at a taxonomy to see how Linnaeus thought about things. This is better than starting with an answer key.

Explanation

There is no 'correct' way to group the plants. This activity should teach children to see differences and to use words that describe different types of plant. It also shows some of the problems associated with classifying plants. It can be done in so many ways! If you look at a normal taxonomy of flora (one that uses the Linnaean system), the plants are not classified in a way that the children or even you might think seems natural and practical. Flowers of the same colour may belong to completely different families. The plants that we call trees are also not always very closely related. However, you might be able to find taxonomies aimed at children, which classify plants in simple ways, such as by colour or where they grow.

Comparing plants

 Divide your piece of paper into two halves by folding it in half and then opening it out.

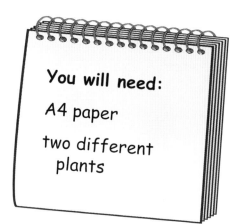

You will need:

A4 paper

two different plants

 Draw one plant on each half. Colour them!

 Find three similarities between the plants.

 Find three differences.

 Write down the similarities and differences you have found.

Comparing plants

Learning objective: to observe and describe similarities and differences between two plants

Curriculum links

England/Wales:	Sc2 3b
Scotland:	KUL B
Northern Ireland:	KLA c

Investigation summary

You will need to bring two different plants into school for the lesson. If it's the right season, you can use two plants from outdoors. Otherwise, shop-bought flowers or potted plants are fine. Children draw the two plants and write down three similarities and three differences.

Tips

If you have some magnifying glasses, it would be interesting for the children to observe the plants up close. Magnification can reveal differences that the naked eye is incapable of seeing. Children looking through a magnifying glass could choose to draw a small section of the plant (a flower or leaf, for example).

Expected results

The drawings are often quite interesting, and can lead to discussions about the differences between and the functions of the various plant parts. To describe differences and similarities among plants, the children need to be able to name the different parts. Be prepared to answer questions about these words.

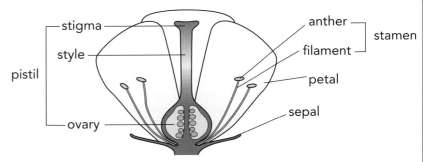

Explanation

To establish order in the great diversity of the plant kingdom, biologists (and other people) use something called plant taxonomy. Plants are sorted into families and groups by appearance or where they grow. Looking very carefully in order to be able to describe later what you've seen is typical of the scientific method. This is what is referred to as making observations. This activity involving two plants is a very simple exercise in observation and description. Observing and carefully drawing plants is by no means a recent idea. Being able to describe medicinal, poisonous and edible plants has always been in people's best interest. There is a long tradition of oral plant knowledge.

Further ideas

Continue this activity by taking children outdoors and asking them to find two different plants, and describe five parts or properties that make the two plants different or similar.

Collecting plants

 Collect some plants from outdoors.

 Arrange them spread out flat on a sheet of newspaper. Try to make them look as nice as possible!

 Place another sheet of newspaper over the top of the plants.

 Place a wooden plank or tray on the newspaper.

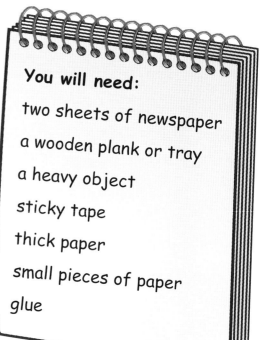

You will need:
two sheets of newspaper
a wooden plank or tray
a heavy object
sticky tape
thick paper
small pieces of paper
glue

 Place something heavy on top of the plank or tray.

 Leave everything as it is for at least two weeks.

 Take the objects off the top, and carefully peel back the top sheet of newspaper.

 Very carefully lift the plants off the bottom sheet of newspaper.

 Tape the plants to a sheet of thick paper.

 Write down some things you know about your plants on small pieces of paper. This could be the name of the plant, where it was growing, when you found it, or anything else you can think of!

 Stick the small pieces of paper next to the plants.

Collecting plants

Learning objective: to learn to recognise some common plants in the local environment

Curriculum links

England/Wales:	Sc2 5a, 5b
Scotland:	KUL A
Northern Ireland:	KLA a

 Make sure children are aware that some plants may be poisonous or trigger allergies, and also that some plants may be protected species. The children should not uproot any plants completely.

Investigation summary

Take children outdoors to find a few plants. Ask children to carefully snip or break off a section of the plant (for example a part of the stem with a single flower and a leaf). Two or three plants is plenty for each child/ group of children. They shouldn't select plants that are too large, wet or hard (for example a rose). Children then press their plants between two sheets of newspaper, with a wooden plank or tray and a heavy object on top. After two weeks, children take their plants out, and display them on thick paper. They write notes about their plants, such as its name, and when and where they found it. Make sure the children know that they do not need to spend ages trying to find out the names of their plants.

Tips

If the plants are wet, the paper should be replaced intermittently during the first few days.

The children could even laminate their dried-plant collages. It would also be nice if they could incorporate them into a plant notebook, which they could use for the duration of the topic.

Expected results

There are usually one or two children who know the names of some of the plants that grow around the school, whilst some of the younger children might still have problems in recognising that it is a plant, and why.

Explanation

A collection of dried plants can also be referred to as a herbarium. This is an age-old method for collecting and sorting plants. Carolus Linnaeus, for example, was very adept at collecting and drying plants. Knowing the full range of plants in the local environment helps us to protect that environment. Sorting plants helps gardeners and conservationists to identify weeds, rare plants and so on.

Further ideas

This is a good opportunity to bring up the topic of endangered species. Try researching on the internet to find details of endangered plants in your area.

Identifying plants

Try to find the correct names of these five plants using the key below.

A  B  C  D  E

 For each plant, start from the left of the key, and decide which statement is true for that plant.

 When you have chosen the best statement, follow the arrow from that statement to the next choice.

 Keep making choices until you reach the name of the plant.

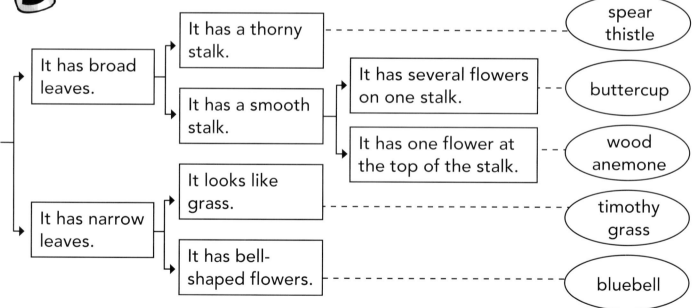

 Write the correct names of the plants.

A _____

B _____

C _____

D _____

E _____

Identifying plants

Learning objective: to use a classification key to help identify plants

Curriculum links

England/Wales:	Sc2 4b;
	KS2 Sc2 4a
Scotland:	KUL C
Northern Ireland:	KLA d, g

Further ideas

You could also try asking the children to gather plants and make their own keys. Pass the keys around and see if they work. To do this successfully, the children will need to come up with their own statements about the appearance of the plants. They will most likely come up with very good, creative suggestions regarding the parts of the plant, colour, leaf shape, where different parts are located, and so on.

Give children leaf identification sheets, and ask them to collect and identify leaves from trees around the school. You can buy leaf identification sheets, download one from several websites (just enter 'leaf identification sheet' into a search engine), or you can make one yourself by drawing or photocopying detailed and accurate pictures of leaves from up to 20 common trees, and printing the name next to each one.

You can perform a wonderful sorting activity using up to 10 different kinds of dried pasta. The pasta can be glued onto large sheets of paper when the sorting is complete.

Investigation summary

Children look carefully at pictures of five plants. They use a key to identify the name of each plant by choosing between pairs of statements until they reach the correct name.

Tips

Some children may have difficulty writing the names, so it is a good idea to provide name labels for them to use.

Expected results

A = timothy grass

B = buttercup

C = wood anemone

D = spear thistle

E = bluebell

Explanation

Most taxonomies of plants (and animals) work this way. You advance along the taxonomic path using a key that presents you with two options to choose from at every step of the way (a branching key). Many excellent computer keys are available and may be useful here. This activity is intended to serve as a simple introduction to how such a key works. It's usually fun to encounter the method in this simplified form. The gap between finding an unknown plant and identifying it in a taxonomy is wide. This activity should spark interest, especially if you let the children make their own keys.

Further investigations

Playing with plants

You will need: a variety of plants; a white cloth; another cloth

Investigation
Option 1: Lay out some well-known plants or plant parts on a white cloth on the ground. Let the children observe the arrangement for about 25 seconds, then cover the plants with another cloth. How many of the plants can the children remember?

Option 2: To be done in two or more groups. Arrange a number of plants or plant parts on a cloth. Lay another cloth over it. When you take the cloth off, tell the children to look closely at them and then go and find similar plants or plant parts outdoors.

Dandelions

You will need: a bunch of dandelions; a ruler

Investigation
Gather a bunch of dandelions and compare them in terms of size, length of stalk, and number of flowers. Measure and count/observe similarities and differences.

Expected results
This exercise demonstrates the great variety found within a single species. It is a good thing that there is so much variation (tall, short, etc.) within the species. This increases the likelihood that some individuals will survive, for example when the lawnmower comes!

Water plants

You will need: some bits of the water plant Elodea (found in pet shops); a plastic or glass jar; water

Investigation
Place the Elodea in a jar full of water. Put the jar in sunlight and see what happens.

Expected results
You'll see bubbles. This is oxygen generated by the plant.

A short history of...
plants

The uses of plants

For a variety of reasons, it has always been absolutely necessary for humans to learn about the plants found on our planet. Such knowledge has been important in finding the best type of tree for building boats and houses, learning how to deal with different types of crop to make them yield food, or finding the types of herb that can cure illness. The earliest known careful biological representations were used to guide early people looking for medicinal herbs.

Carolus Linnaeus

One of the Swedish naturalist Carolus Linnaeus's (1707–1778) most brilliant and revolutionary ideas was that plants also have sex lives. He was only 22 when he claimed that plants have sexual organs. He carefully studied the parts of plants, describing the pistils as female and the stamens as male. This was entirely at odds with the thinking of the day. People did not think of plants as sexual beings.

Linnaeus also developed a workable system for classifying plants, and came up with an intelligent way of naming all plants. He named them in Latin. As in a telephone book, his system organises them by last name (genus name), followed by the species name. For example, *Primula veris* is the latin name for a cowslip. This was a welcome contribution to botanists around the world. Now there was a language to work with that everyone could understand. One no longer needed to learn the names that every other country used for the same flower. The system Linnaeus later launched in his writings was based on careful study of the various parts of the flower. The entire plant kingdom was classified by the number of pistils, which remains in effect to this day. It is a simple and easily comprehensible system.

Current research into plants

These days, now that we know that genes are the carriers of traits, researchers are using what is referred to as genetic manipulation to design the crops of the future. This is a hotly debated topic, especially when it comes to the plants that we eat. It is possible to mix and match plant properties almost at random, for example mixing fish genes with those of a tree to make better wood. It is possible to grow grapes that taste like strawberries and apples that taste awful!

Animals

Investigation	Curriculum links

Classroom investigations

Sorting animals
to sort and classify various animals

Sc2 4b: group living things according to observable similarities and differences
KUL A: sort living things into broad groups according to easily observable characteristics
KLA d: sort living things into groups using observable features

Spiders and webs
to study spiders and webs closely and compare them to previous understanding

Sc2 1c: to relate life processes to animals and plants found in the local environment
KUL A: recognise and name some common plants and animals found in the local environment
KLA f: find out about some animals, including how they grow, feed, move and use their senses

Minibeast hunt
to study a minibeast closely

Sc2 1c: to relate life processes to animals and plants found in the local environment
KUL A: recognise and name some common plants and animals found in the local environment
KLA a: find out about the variety of animal and plant life both through direct observations and by using secondary sources

Building an animal
to construct a model of an animal and describe its appearance and characteristics

Sc1 2a: ask questions and decide how they might find answers to them
SIS B: make suggestions about what might happen
INP b: talk about what they are going to make and the materials they will use

Further investigations

Minibeast trap

Slugs and snails

Facts about...

animals

The animal kingdom

The animal kingdom is amazingly diverse. Today we know of around 1.5 million species, but there may be just as many awaiting discovery. People throughout the ages have been interested in determining how various animals are related to each other. This was very important knowledge in the breeding of domestic animals.

Invertebrates and vertebrates

According to the classification of the animal kingdom we use today, the kingdom is divided into two main groups. The first group consists of invertebrates (animals without a spinal column). Some of these species have no skeleton at all, while others have an exoskeleton. Ninety-five per cent of all species belong to this group. The other large group consists of vertebrates, which includes all animals with an internal skeleton (endoskeleton). To be able to classify an animal correctly, one has to make very careful observations. Two species may differ by a very small detail. Sometimes the number of legs is what determines what group the animal belongs to; sometimes it is something about how the animal breathes.

From protozoa to human beings

The entire classification of the animal kingdom mirrors the process of evolution. The simplest and most primitive types of animal were also the first types to appear on earth. It is from these simple forms that higher life forms, including humankind, have developed over the course of millions of years.

Natural selection

Charles Darwin's theory of evolution was an attempt to explain the origin of species. Based on observations made in nature, he suggested that life's development is governed by something called natural selection. There exists an interplay of an organism's genes and the environment in which it lives, which may lead to adaptations whereby those who are the most successful in obtaining food have the greatest chance of propagating their traits. This is how their genes are passed on.

The moth that changed colour

Here is an example that sheds light on one of the mechanisms behind evolution. As recently as 200 years ago, nearly all peppered moths in England were white. This provided excellent camouflage, making them hard to see against birch bark. Dark moths were easier prey for predators. Due to the advance of industrial civilisation in the 1800s and the widespread coal combustion that accompanied it, enough sooty pollution entered the air to turn the birch trunks black. This favoured moths that were born black. Since this characteristic suddenly became helpful to the species, most peppered moths eventually came to be black. Now that coal combustion has been kerbed and birch bark has reverted to its white colour, it is again the white moths that are favoured. They are now the ones with the highest survival rate and thus the most offspring. This is evolution by natural selection.

SAFARI PARK

Meena and Jamie are at a safari park.

Come and look at this, Meena!

Sea Cucumber

Sea Tulip

Are they plants or animals?

I think the sea cucumber is an animal. The sea tulip is... umm...

Later, Jamie and Meena are looking at the monkeys.

I know that monkeys are animals.

They like eatings plants.

Ha ha ha!

Ha ha ha!

Umm, Jamie... there's a spider on your arm. Shoo!

I wonder if we could move that fast if we had eight legs...

Notes on the story

Plant or animal?

There are many animals with confusing names: tiger-lily, stick insect, dogwood, hedgehog, grass snake, cowslip, catkin, cabbage white. What is 'typical' of animals and plants? Some might suggest that animals have children, but plants do not. Yet there are many examples of animals, such as amoebas, that reproduce just by splitting in half. Another suggestion is that animals have mouths and plants have roots. Yet many plants have no roots, absorbing water through their 'bodies' instead, and some appear to eat, such as the venus flytrap.

The monkey

Jamie and Meena's conversation about the monkey contains a hint about what makes plants and animals different. All animals ultimately derive their nutrition from green plants. Green plants contain chlorophyll. This substance helps harness the energy of the Sun and make energy-rich compounds using such simple substances as carbon dioxide and water. This process is called photosynthesis, and its result is sugar. Herbivores eat plants, and carnivores may eat other animals who eat plants.

The bird

The bird has eaten fruits and seeds from trees and bushes (green plants). After digesting the food, the parrot excretes any remaining material that the body has not used. This waste contains substances that are very useful to plants.

How many legs?

Different creatures have a different number of legs, and they can move in very different ways. Humans can walk forwards, backwards and sideways, but other bipeds cannot. Quadrupeds have many different ways of walking: compare a cat and a horse, for example. Six-legged creatures, such as ants, walk in a sort of triangle pattern: they firstly move the front and back legs on one side and the middle leg on the other side, and then switch sides. Eight-legged creatures, such as spiders, move one leg at a time.

Sorting animals

 Cut out the pictures below.

 Sort the animals into groups that you think make sense.

 Write down what the animals in each of your groups have in common.

 Compare your groups to what other children in the class have done.

You will need:
scissors

cow	lynx	worm	fish
starfish	dolphin	gorilla	eagle
butterfly	frog	ostrich	crocodile
grasshopper	blue tit	snake	human

Sorting animals

Learning objective: to sort and classify various animals

Curriculum links

England/Wales:	Sc2 4b
Scotland:	KUL A
Northern Ireland:	KLA d

Investigation summary

Children cut out the 16 pictures of animals and sort them into groups that they think are appropriate. They then write down what they think the animals in each of their groups have in common. They compare their system of classification with that of others in the class. This activity can be conducted either individually or in groups. Encourage different types of solution. Summarise all the different suggestions in a class discussion.

Tips

It is a good idea to enlarge the pictures using a photocopier.

Expected results

The children may arrange the animals by where they live, their colour, if they can fly, how many legs they have, whether they live in water, whether they have legs, and so on. Some children may sort them into mammals, insects, birds, amphibians, reptiles and fish.

Explanation

Animals can of course be sorted in many different ways. One common way is to group them by where they live. Another way, developed by the Swede Carolus Linnaeus, is used by biologists around the world to classify animals. Here is how the cards would be arranged according to that system:

Vertebrates

Cow, lynx, dolphin, gorilla, human *(mammals)*

Eagle, ostrich, blue tit *(birds)*

Crocodile, snake *(reptiles)*

Frog *(amphibian)*

Fish

Invertebrates

Butterfly, grasshopper *(insects)*

Worm

Starfish *(echinoderm)*

Animal taxonomies usually use a similar system. Try researching this on the internet or at a local wildlife centre.

Spiders and webs

 Divide your two sheets of paper by folding them in half and then opening them out.

 On one half of the first sheet, draw what you think a spider looks like. Make it big and clear!

 On one half of the other sheet, draw what you think a spider's web looks like.

You will need:

two sheets of paper

a small jar with a lid, or a pooter

a magnifying glass

 Go outside and find some spiders and spider webs.

 Look very closely at a web and draw it next to your first web drawing.

 Catch a spider and study it with a magnifying glass.

 Draw it next to your first spider drawing.

What differences do you *see between* your first and second drawings?

 Compare your spider to the spiders caught by other children in the class.

What differences can *you see* between your spider and theirs?

Is there anything *else* you'd like to find out about spiders and their webs?

 Write down your questions and thoughts.

Spiders and webs

Learning objective: to study spiders and webs closely and compare them to previous understanding

Curriculum links

England/Wales: Sc2 1c

Scotland: KUL A

Northern Ireland: KLA f

Investigation summary

Children draw pictures of what they think a spider and a spider web look like. Then take the children outside to look at some actual spiders and webs. They should find a spider and a web, study them closely, and then draw them next to their previous drawings. They will need small jars with lids or, if possible, pooters. A pooter is a device scientists use to pick up insects without hurting them. It is a small pot with two tubes going into it; children hold one tube over the insect they want to catch, and suck through the other tube. The suction draws the insect into the pot. Be sure to explain carefully which tube the children should suck through!

Tips

Finding spiders is usually not difficult. Lift up stones and look in nooks and crannies. If you are outside, it's best to go where it is warm and dry. To see the spider webs you've found more clearly, you can spray them with a plant mister.

Do make sure that the children ventilate the jars now and then. Take care of the spiders and release them once you are finished with them.

Expected results

This well-known creature turns out to have many things about it awaiting discovery. How many legs does it have? How many body parts? Does it have antennae? Does it have eyes? Does it have a mouth? How big is the web? By first asking the children to draw what they think a spider looks like, you should spark the children's eagerness to find out the details they do not know.

Explanation

Spiders are arachnids, a class of arthropod, not insects. They have two main body parts, and all eight legs are attached to the front part. The front part also has eight single-lens eyes. A spider does not have antennae, but it does have sensory organs by the mouth called palps. Its mouth has mandibles, but no stinger. The abdomen has silk glands that contain a fluid that hardens into very durable fibres when it hits the air. The material in spider webs is five times stronger than steel and 30% more elastic than nylon. Spiders are predators, and to eat their prey they inject them with a digestive juice and then suck out the resulting slurry.

Minibeast hunt

 Go outside and find some minibeasts!

 Capture the one you want to study. Scoop it very gently into your jar, or hold the correct tube of your pooter over it and suck it into the container!

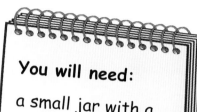

You will need:

a small jar with a lid, or a pooter

a magnifying glass

scissors

 Draw the minibeast you've captured. Try to note all the details.

 Colour your picture.

What is your minibeast doing?

What parts can you see?

 Describe your minibeast to a friend.

Minibeast hunt

Learning objective: to study a minibeast closely

Curriculum links

England/Wales:	Sc2 1c
Scotland:	KUL A
Northern Ireland:	KLA a

Investigation summary

Take the children outdoors and ask them to search for minibeasts. Provide them with small jars with lids, or pooters if you have them. When each child/group of children finds a minibeast they are interested in, they should capture it in their jar or pooter. They then bring it back to the classroom to observe, draw and describe it. Don't forget to release the minibeasts afterwards!

Tips

Good places to look include under rocks or tufts of grass, especially in moist, shady places. Don't allow the children to put more than one minibeast in the same jar or pooter – to avoid cannibalism! If the minibeasts are moving around too much for children to study them, you can put the container, with the creature inside, onto an ice cube for a minute (but no longer). The creature will then move more slowly. This should not harm them!

Expected results

Here are some examples of the minibeasts that can be caught using a pooter: beetles, earwigs, millipedes, centipedes, flies, spiders, woodlice. The parts of the creatures that are usually visible include legs, antennae, eyes, wings and mouth.

Building an animal

 Build an animal – it can be imaginary or real!
Use things from the list, or anything
else your teacher gives you.

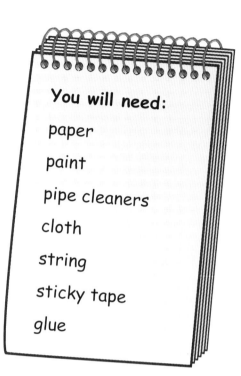

You will need:
paper
paint
pipe cleaners
cloth
string
sticky tape
glue

 Think about these questions:
How big will your animal be?
How many legs will it have?
What will its eyes be like?
What is it called?
Where does it live?
What does it eat?

 'Interview' your animal, and then tell a friend about it!
Use the following questions, and any others you can think of.

Where do you live?
What do you eat?
What does your home look like?
Do you have any relatives?
How do you protect yourself against enemies?

Building an animal

Learning objective: to construct a model of an animal and describe its appearance and characteristics

Curriculum links

England/Wales:	Sc1 2a
Scotland:	SIS B
Northern Ireland:	INP b

Investigation summary

Provide children with materials for building animals of their choice. They each decide what their animal should look like and what characteristics it should have. Allow them free rein for this, but you may want to encourage them to think about reasons for each feature: does it need to be able to run fast, pick up heavy things, climb trees, and so on. Children pretend to 'interview' their animal, and then tell a classmate the answers to the questions.

Expected results

The results are usually beautiful and full of creativity!

Further investigations

Minibeast trap

You will need: some jars; planks of wood

Investigation

Bury the jars in the soil in a few different places around the school. The tops of the jars should be level with the top of the soil. Put some soil, grass and leaves in the bottom of each jar and then cover with a plank of wood, or it will get too wet if it rains. Prop up the ends of the plank on small stones so that there is a small space between the plank and the top of the jar.

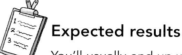

Expected results

You'll usually end up with a good catch! You may find a lot of beetles to draw and study. The ground abounds with minibeasts; there are legions of tiny creatures under each footstep! Scientists have calculated that when an adult takes a walk through the forest, at any one time he may be treading on 19000 mites, 400 tiny ringworms, 1500 springtails, 20 millipedes, 70 fly larvae, 10 spiders and 100000 nematodes. There are also many billions of bacteria.

Slugs and snails

You will need: a snail or slug; a magnifying glass; a sheet of glass or acrylic; a ruler; a stopwatch

Investigation

Collect snails or slugs and study them. Let the children ask questions and try to answer them by studying the animals. Let the slug/snail slide over a sheet of glass or acrylic. This will give you a good look at the underside of the slug/snail. How do they reproduce? (They are hermaphrodites – each individual is both male and female, but two slugs/snails are needed for reproduction to take place.) What do they eat? (They are vegetarians. You can see the mouth parts through the glass.) Find out how fast they move using a ruler and stopwatch.

Further ideas

People say that snails like to eat mail! You could set the class the challenge of finding out if this is true – and if so, what sort of envelopes they like best!

A short history of...
animals

Cave paintings

In the caves of southern Europe, paintings have been found that represent bison and other animals. These paintings were made by people who lived in the Neolithic period around 25 000 BC. They most likely made them in order to learn more about the animals that represented their most important food source. Just as today's naturalists do, they carefully studied the animals' habits and behaviour – not to write about them and classify them into groups, but to make it easier to catch them.

Microscopic life

When scientists started gaining access to microscopes, proof to refute Aristotle's ideas started piling up. By the beginning of the 1700s, it was obvious that life cannot just 'appear' out of food scraps. Using ever more effective tools, they were able to glimpse into the previously unknown world of microscopic life. Soon, research into the animal world was advancing by leaps and bounds, with some scientists spending their entire lives studying micro-organisms under a microscope. Riddles as to the origin of many diseases were solved. Sterilisation and antiseptic methods were used to halt the spread of disease. Doctors performing surgery began washing their hands – before operating!

Aristotle and the animal world

One of the first people to attempt a systematic description and classification of animals was Aristotle of ancient Greece (383–322 BC). He was a very wise man, and many students eager for knowledge joined his school. He divided the animal world into 11 classes. He also compared development across bird species. Aristotle proposed some ideas about reproduction. For instance, he believed that flies spawned spontaneously out of rotten meat – that they came 'from nowhere' inside the meat. This false idea about spontaneous generation survived for a very long time.

Linnaeus named the animals

When Carolus Linnaeus released the 10th edition of his ground-breaking book *Systemae Naturae* in 1758, he broadened his work to include animals as well as plants. He used his brilliant system to name every animal in Latin, just as he had the plants. For instance, all cats originally had names that begin with *Felis*, for example a domestic cat was *Felis catur*, a tiger was *Felis tigris*, and a lion was *Felis leo*. More recently, further distinctions have been made, so that big cats are now in a different category, *Panthera*, and the tiger is known as *Panthera tigris*.

Everything can be sorted

 Investigation   **Curriculum links**

Classroom investigations

What's inside?
to use appropriate words to describe properties

Sc1 1: Pupils should be taught that it is important to collect evidence by making observations and measurements when trying to answer a question
SIS A: make suggestions and contribute to the planning of simple practical explorations
INP c: ask questions, discuss ideas and make predictions

What is it made of?
to describe different materials based on their properties and to think about their origins

Sc3 1a: use their senses to explore and recognise the similarities and differences between materials
KUE B: make observations of differences in the properties of common materials
KMP c: explore the properties of materials including shape, colour, texture and behaviour

What's in the jar?
to classify different substances by their properties

Sc3 1b: sort objects into groups on the basis of simple material properties
KUE B: make observations of differences in the properties of common materials
KMP b: sort a range of everyday objects into groups according to the materials from which they are made
KMP c: explore the properties of materials including shape, colour, texture and behaviour

Fruit salad
to use careful observation to describe and classify substances based on their properties

Sc3 1b: sort objects into groups on the basis of simple material properties
KUE B: make observations of differences in the properties of common materials
KMP b: sort a range of everyday objects into groups according to the materials from which they are made
KMP c: explore the properties of materials including shape, colour, texture and behaviour

Sorting in a jar
to sort objects according to whether they float or sink

Sc3 1b: sort objects into groups on the basis of simple material properties
KUE B: make observations of differences in the properties of common materials
KMP b: sort a range of everyday objects into groups according to the materials from which they are made
KMP c: explore the properties of materials including shape, colour, texture and behaviour

Modelling dough and water
to investigate why objects float or sink

Sc3 1c: recognise and name common types of material and recognise that some of them are found naturally
KUE A: recognise and name some common materials from living and non-living sources
KUE B: make observations of differences in the properties of common materials
KMP b: sort a range of everyday objects into groups according to the materials from which they are made
KMP c: explore the properties of materials including shape, colour, texture and behaviour

Home investigations

Does it sink or float?

Further investigations

Sorting buttons

A potato in water

58

Facts about...
substances, elements and atoms

Scientists believe that all the matter in the universe was formed by the Big Bang. The stars and moon, your football and the apple chunks in your fruit salad all have the same origin. Matter consists of many different elements. Scientists have always classified elements by their properties, described them and named them. Chemists are always looking for new substances with new properties, that can be used in different ways: metal to forge, rock to build with, paints with which to paint, plastics to make things etc.

Atoms: the building blocks of nature

Among other things, the classification of substances has led to the knowledge that all matter (everything around us) consists of atoms. Atoms are incredibly small building blocks. Atoms are so small that they cannot be seen. If you were to enlarge an atom to the size of a marble, and you then enlarged the marble by the same amount, the marble would have a diameter of 500 km!

Different types of atom

There are only about a hundred different kinds of atom. But they can be combined and bonded to each other in endless ways to create different compounds and substances. What differentiates one type of atom from another is that it contains a differing number of particles. On earth, we are stuck with the atoms we have. The same atoms are used again and again. An atom from what used to be a hedgehog might be found in a table today!

The elements

Substances that consist of a single type of atom are called elements. Since there are only a hundred or so different kinds of atom, there are only a hundred or so elements. All these elements have their own unique properties. Elements can react with each other to form chemical bonds. There are approximately 10.5 million known chemical bonds on earth.

Iron is an element. It contains only iron atoms.

This iron is a combination of many different kinds of atom!

A VISIT TO THE SUPERMARKET

Jamie and Meena visit the supermarket.

Someone has dropped something! What is it?

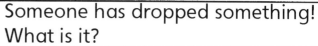

It is flour!

There is washing powder on the floor. Who spilt it?

It was the dog!

Watch out, Meena!

Notes on the story

Supermarket shelves

This chapter is about describing and classifying everyday objects based on their properties. In a supermarket, everything is arranged by type. Look at the fruit and vegetable sections for instance. Ask children to think about what characteristics are used for sorting the products. This is good practice for finding the words to describe various properties.

Similar substances

Lots of things that can be found in a supermarket look very similar when they are not in their packets, for example washing powder, sugar, salt and baking soda. Some are very fine, others are more coarse. You have to use your senses: smell, touch and sight.

Sink or float

One way to classify substances is by investigating whether they sink or float in various liquids. Different substances behave differently due to varying density. There are many examples in the supermarket: olives in water, fruit in syrup and cream in milk, for example.

What's inside?

1 Try to find out what is inside the lump of dough!
You may stick the matchstick into the dough
10 times at different angles – but not too hard!
You may not try to change the shape of the lump of dough.

You will need:

a lump of modelling dough with something hidden inside

a used matchstick

2 Draw what you think the object inside looks like.

3 Describe what it feels like in words.

4 Take the object out from inside the dough.

Were you right? Compare the object to your drawing.

5 Draw the actual object.

What's inside?

Learning objective: to use appropriate words to describe properties

Curriculum links

England/Wales	Sc1 1
Scotland:	SIS A
Northern Ireland:	INP c

Investigation summary

Hide small objects in round lumps of modelling dough about 5 cm in diameter. Give pairs or groups of children one each. They use a spent matchstick to probe the object by sticking it in 10 times at different angles. Ask questions to help them, if necessary, for example 'What does it feel like? Is it heavier or lighter than expected? What shape does it have?' They draw and describe how they think the object looks and feels, and then compare the actual object with their guess.

Tips

Use different coloured lumps of dough to help you keep track of what is hidden inside each lump. Good things to hide are pieces of plastic of various shapes, peas, screws, keys, stones, acorns, nuts, or marbles. It is a good idea to hide some easy and some difficult objects. Don't hide things that might break when poked with a match!

Expected results

Some children will guess their objects, and others won't. You will hear lots of creative suggestions and fanciful ideas! The purpose of this exercise is partly to communicate the importance of making careful, accurate and relevant observations to support ideas and predictions, and partly to encourage the children to reason and express their ideas verbally. It is important to give them an opportunity to formulate their ideas and communicate their observations both verbally and graphically. It is also a good idea to give them a chance to discuss their ideas with their classmates.

Further ideas

There are many good hypothesis exercises. Instead of a lump of modelling dough, you can hide objects in small boxes, and mount two sticks in holes as 'feelers'.

You might draw a comparison between this activity and how chemists and scientists use their tools to investigate a microscopic world to see what atoms look like and what they are composed of. Based on their observations, scientists formulate hypotheses to describe what they think atoms look like.

What is it made of?

 Look around the classroom for objects made from different materials.

 Look carefully at each object.
Feel them and smell them!
Describe each object to your partner.

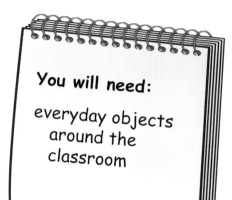
You will need:

everyday objects around the classroom

What types of word will you use to describe the objects?

 Draw each object and write down what materials it is made of.

Why do you think these materials were chosen to make each object?

Do you know anything about where these materials come from?

Do you know anything about how these materials are made?

What do you think happens to these things when we do not want them any more?

What is it made of?

Learning objective: to describe different materials based on their properties and to think about their origins

Curriculum links

England/Wales:	Sc3 1a
Scotland:	KUE B
Northern Ireland:	KMP c

 Make sure the children take care when sniffing objects. Do not let them put their noses too close.

Further ideas

Make a display of different types of material. Set up a table with different everyday objects that the children bring to school. Discuss the objects, what they are made of and what they are used for. Extend the discussion about uses of materials. Ask questions such as: 'Why do you think so many toys are made of plastic? What do you think are the properties that help a mop to do its job? What do you think is the most useful material in the classroom?' Find examples of different materials that serve the same purpose, for example keeping us warm, containing drinks, covering floors.

If possible, you could arrange for a fabric specialist or wood- or metal-worker to visit the school, to talk to the children about the origins and applications of textiles, woods or metals.

 ## Investigation summary

Allow children to wander freely around the classroom to find everyday objects. Children describe their chosen objects to their partner. Give the children plenty of time to think and discuss. Let them feel and smell the various materials. Children then draw the objects and write what materials each one is made of. They should think about where the materials come from, how they are made, and what happens to them when they are no longer needed.

Tips

Conduct this activity with the classroom just the way it is. There are plenty of different types of material around you without preparing anything special!

 ## Expected results

Here are some suggestions regarding materials found in a typical classroom:

table: hard, smooth, opaque; made of wood; comes from trees

window: hard, transparent, cold; made of glass; comes from melted sand

ruler: hard, flexible; made of plastic; made in factories.

Explanation

The types of material we use in a typical classroom depend on many different factors (cost, tradition, functionality). The suitability of different materials for recycling is something that is being discussed more and more. Whether certain types of material (such as building materials) provoke allergies is also coming under increasing scrutiny.

What's in the jar?

 Look at the contents of each jar.

 Use all your senses to work out what it is. Only taste a very tiny bit!

 Describe each substance.

You will need:

numbered jars containing different things

a large sheet of paper or a tray

Can you name any of the *substances*?

Are any of the *substances* similar in *some way*?

 Try to sort the substances into different groups.

 Make a drawing or a table to show how you sorted the substances.

What's in the jar?

Learning objective: to classify different substances by their properties

Curriculum links

England/Wales:	Sc3 1b
Scotland:	KUE B
Northern Ireland:	KMP b, c

Everything in the jars must be safe to eat. Make sure the children only taste a tiny bit. Watch out for children with food allergies.

Investigation summary

Fill at least 10 glass jars with different substances. Label each jar and number it. Make a note of which substance is in each jar! Try to fill the jars with substances that look similar, such as flour, salt, sugar, citric acid, tartaric acid, baking soda. Other ideas are water and other liquids, or cereal grains. Keep the set of jars on your desk or a central table and allow children to take one jar at a time. In groups, they examine and describe each substance, try to work out what they are, and then sort them into groups, perhaps using sorting circles. They draw a picture or table to show how they decided to sort the substances. Discuss together the classification choices made by the children.

Expected results

The children will be able to identify the contents of some of the jars quite easily, but the point is for them to practise describing their observations verbally, using words such as slippery, soft, shiny, sticky, hard, transparent, smelly, bright, flexible. Some substances are difficult to recognise. The senses unaided are not enough.

You will hear many different suggestions as to how to classify the substances. Some children may suggest that substances found in the kitchen belong together, but others may sort by colour, solids and liquids, solubility in water, or whether it 'grows'. Oppositions such as natural/artificial or imported/British may also come into play. There are no clear-cut answers here!

Explanation

Where the senses alone are not sufficient, we must refer to more scientific approaches. For example, we could test whether substances are magnetic, at what temperature they change state, whether they are water-soluble, or whether they conduct electricity.

Everyday example

The sorting of rubbish is an important example of the need to classify substances accurately.

Fruit salad

 Put three tablespoons of fruit salad on your plate.

 Try to name the fruits in the salad without tasting them!

 Draw and write what you think the ingredients are.

You will need:
fruit salad
a tablespoon
a paper plate
a toothpick

Fruit salad

Learning objective: to use careful observation to describe, compare and classify substances based on their properties

Curriculum links

England/Wales:	Sc3 1b
Scotland:	KUE B
Northern Ireland:	KMP b, c

Investigation summary

Prepare in advance a bowl of fruit salad. The fruit should be cut into very small pieces, so that each fruit is not easily recognisable. Use as many different fruits (and vegetables, if you like!) as you can. The fruit salad should also contain things that are hard to find without resorting to scientific methods, for example lemon juice, ascorbic acid, cinnamon. It is a good idea for children to work in small groups. Each group should put three tablespoons of the salad on a paper plate. They should try to work out all the ingredients in the salad by using all their senses except for taste! They draw and describe what they think the ingredients are. Encourage the children to see similarities and differences among the ingredients. You can help them by pointing out certain details. It is useful to have a magnifying glass handy.

Tips

You can use a tin of fruit salad as your base to save time. Keep the tin so you have a record of what it contains.

Expected results

Some of the fruits are easy to recognise based on their smell and consistency, but others may be more difficult. It is also difficult to detect dissolved sugar, lemon juice and other less visible substances. If you use tinned fruit salad as your base, on the label you will find listed some substances that cannot be recognised by sight, smell or touch. The senses are not sensitive enough to distinguish these.

Explanation

What we are looking for here is the recipe for the fruit salad. This investigation paints a picture of how chemists throughout the ages have sought the 'recipe' of how the world works, or the ingredients in the greatest and most mysterious dish ever made: The Universe! Explain to the children that chemists have to be very careful when investigating substances that they do not recognise. It would be very foolish to establish the identity of a toxic or corrosive substance by means of a taste test!

Further ideas

A good end to this exercise would be to serve a fresh, 'uninvestigated' fruit salad for everyone to eat at the end of the class!

Sorting in a jar

 Look at all the objects you have in front of you.

How do you think it would look if you put all these things into the jar?

 Draw a picture to show what you think will happen.

 Pour the cooking oil into the jar.

 Pour the syrup into the jar.

 Pour the cold water into the jar.

 Add the other things one by one. Don't shake the jar!

 Draw a picture of the contents of the jar.

Why do you think this has happened?

You will need:

cold water

syrup

cooking oil

a screw

a piece of dried pasta

a chunk of potato

a chunk of apple

the end of a candle

a large, empty, glass jar

Sorting in a jar

Learning objective: to sort objects according to whether they float or sink

Curriculum links

England/Wales:	Sc3 1b
Scotland:	KUE B
Northern Ireland:	KMP b, c

Investigation summary

The children think about what a mixture of substances will look like when put together in a jar. They draw a picture to show their thinking. They add all the ingredients, and draw what it looks like. You could also ask children what they think will happen if the substances are added in a different order. Many children believe this will yield different results. Model this investigation for them, to show that the order in which the substances are added makes no difference.

Tips

Use a tall jar and add plenty of the liquids, at least 200 ml each, so that the results are clear. Use cold water to stop the syrup dissolving. The syrup should be dark, but transparent. The chunks of fruit should be approximately 1 cm³. Use a type of pasta that is not hollow. This investigation is a good one to run as a demonstration. Arrange the objects for everyone to see, and let different children come up and participate.

Everyday example

Ask children to think about things in the kitchen that have different layers, for example salad dressings that contain oil and vinegar.

Expected results

If you use the items listed in the instructions, the results will be as follows:

oil — water — syrup — apple — candle — pasta — potato — screw

Further ideas

You can highlight the idea of density from two different angles:
1 Take equal-sized cubes of different materials, for example plastic, wood and polystyrene. Let the children feel that some feel heavier, even though they are the same size.
2 Take pieces of different materials that each have the same mass. Demonstrate using a set of scales that they each weigh the same. The children will be able to see that they are different sizes.

Explanation

Children will often think that the oil floats on the water because it is lighter, but this is only half the story. You can demonstrate this using two identical jars, one containing 100 ml of cooking oil and one containing 100 ml of water. Emphasise that the volume of each substance is the same. Ask children to predict which jar will weigh more (have more mass). Use a balance to test their predictions. They will see that 100 ml of water has more mass than 100 ml of oil. This is because the oil has less 'stuff' per unit volume (it is less dense). Now add more oil to the jar until the balance shows that the oil is heavier than the water. Pour the water on top of the oil. Children will see that despite being heavier, the oil will float on the water, because it is less dense. The other substances float at different heights because they also have different densities.

Modelling dough and water

 1 Place your lump of modelling dough in the bowl of water.

Does it float?

 **You will need:**

a lump of modelling dough

a bowl or tub of water

paper clips

 2 Try changing the shape of the dough, and testing each to see if it floats.

What is the best shape you can give the dough to make it float?

 3 Draw a picture of the shape.

 4 If you have found a shape that floats, try putting one paper clip at a time on top of the dough.

Does it still float? How many paper clips can you add?

 5 Draw what you see and write down the highest number of paper clips you added.

Modelling dough and water

Learning objective: to investigate why objects float or sink

Curriculum links

England/Wales:	Sc3 1c
Scotland:	KUE A, B
Northern Ireland:	KMP b, c

Investigation summary

Give each group of children a round ball of modelling dough. Show them that each ball weighs the same. Children change the shape of the lump of modelling dough to see if they can find a shape that floats in water. They are not allowed to add or take away any dough. Once they have made a floating shape, they can try loading their 'boat' with paper clips, adding them carefully one at a time, and observing what happens.

Tips

It is best to use transparent bowls or tubs. If you don't have any small paper clips for the children to load onto their floating shapes, find some other light objects, such as staples. It is important to use objects of exactly the same weight. This teaches children how to measure, and shows the need for standardised units.

Expected results

If the modelling dough is shaped like a ball, it will sink. If it is flattened out and slightly curved, it will float. The number of paper clips needed to sink the boat will vary for many reasons, for example the size of the lump of dough, its shape, how thin it has been stretched. This would make an interesting side investigation: puzzlingly, a larger, and therefore heavier, piece of dough can be made into a boat with a greater carrying capacity.

Explanation

The shape of an object affects its ability to float in water. The boat-shaped modelling dough floats because it has less mass than the amount of water it displaces. When it is loaded with paper clips, the boat will sink when the combined mass of modelling dough and paper clips is greater than that of the water they displace.

Everyday examples

Many ships are made of steel, a substance which we normally think of as too 'heavy' to float.

Further ideas

Another good material to investigate is glass. A glass marble does not float in water, but an empty glass bottle will float. The glass bottle will sink when it is filled with water.

Home investigation

Does it sink or float?

You will need:

a jar filled with water

two different-sized
  chunks of apple

two different-sized
  chunks of raw potato

a tea light in metal casing

a square of foil

 Put the two pieces of apple in the jar of water.

 Put the two pieces of potato in the jar.

 Take the metal casing off the tea light and put
the candle in the jar.

Which *objects* float?

 Draw a picture of the jar with all the objects in the water.
Make sure you draw each object in the correct position!

Why do you think this happens?

 Take the objects out of the jar. Place the empty metal casing on top
of the water so it floats. Then slowly pour water into the casing.

What happened? Can you explain why?

 Carefully curve the square of foil to make a shallow 'bowl'.
Place it gently on top of the water.

What happened?

 Take the foil out and crumple it up into a very tight ball.

Do you think this will float or sink?

 Place the ball of foil in the water.

What happens? Can you explain why?

Home investigation teacher notes

Does it sink or float?

Investigation summary

Children place different objects in a jar of water to see which ones float, and at what heights: different-sized chunks of apple and potato, and a small candle (a tea light). They try floating the empty metal casing from the tea light, and see what happens when they fill it with water. Finally they try putting a square of aluminium foil curved into a shallow 'bowl' shape in the water, and then try it with the foil scrunched tightly into a ball.

Expected results

Whatever the size of the potato chunks, they will sink in water. The apple chunks will float relatively high in the water. The candle will float quite low down. The metal casing will float easily, but the more water is added, the lower it will float, until at last it sinks. The foil 'bowl' shape will float as long as it doesn't break the surface tension of the water, but the tight ball of foil will sink.

Explanation

Whether a material floats or sinks in water depends largely on its density. The way something floats or sinks can also be affected by its shape. For example, if the metal casing were flat, it would displace very little water and would sink. The foil floats when it is curved into a 'bowl' shape because it has less mass than the water it displaces. It sinks when it is in a tight ball because it displaces much less water.

Further investigations

Sorting buttons

You will need: lots of different buttons

Investigation

Ask the children to sort the buttons into groups. They should explain their classification verbally, describing why they think certain buttons should go together. They should then draw a picture or diagram to record their grouping.

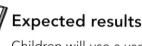

Expected results

Children will use a variety of different ways to describe properties of objects, and the differences between them. There will be a large range of ideas about classifying them, for example by colour, material, number of holes, size, shape, and so on.

> **Further ideas**
> Shoes are another good example of something children can classify (size, waterproof or not, warmth, style, traction, etc.).

A potato in water

Although this investigation is about density, it is an interesting extension of the 'Does it sink or float?' investigation on pages 74 and 75.

You will need: a glass jar filled with water; a potato; salt; a spoon

Investigation

Children observe how a potato floats in water. First, they put the potato in plain water. Then, they add lots of salt and see what happens. They may need to stir with a spoon to dissolve the salt. Alternatively, children could place the potato in a large, transparent container filled with salty water, then keep adding water until the potato begins to sink.

Expected results

The potato sinks in the plain water, but will float when salt is dissolved in the water. With just the right amount of salt, the potato will float in the middle of the jar.

Explanation

The potato is denser than the plain water, so the potato sinks. A solution of water and salt is denser than the potato, so the potato floats.

A short history of...
the earliest chemists

How it all started

Humans began a very long time ago to make use of the different properties of materials to increase their chances of survival. They used hard, sharp stones to cut the hide off animals they had hunted. They used clay to make vessels to store food. They also used clay, soot and minerals to make pigments, which they used to paint cave pictures.

The first attempts at an explanation

The Greek philosophers were the first people to properly try to explain why different substances behaved the way they did when they were heated, oxidised or evaporated. Among them was Thales of Miletos (7th century BC), whose ideas were based on the assumption that all matter was derived from a primary substance: water. Empedocles came up with a different theory in about 450 BC. He claimed that all matter was made up of various combinations of what he called the four elements: earth, air, fire and water.

Modern chemistry

Jan Baptise van Helmont (1577–1644) realised that fire was not an element, but consisted of glowing particles. Robert Boyle (1627–1691) classified matter into elements and chemical compounds. Joseph Black (1728–1799) showed that the gas we now call carbon dioxide is found in the air we breathe.

The biggest step taken in the new direction taken by chemistry is often attributed to the Frenchman Antoine Laurent Lavoisier (1743–1794). At the time, many people believed that heat was a substance with mass, but Lavoisier succeeded, by bold hypotheses and careful measurements, to prove this theory wrong. In 1789, he published a monograph containing a list of 33 chemical elements.

The discovery of atoms and elements

As long ago as 400 BC, the ancient Greek Demokritos said that matter consisted of tiny indivisible parts, which he called atoms. He was certainly on the right track, but we now know that atoms are made up of even smaller parts.

In 1807, the Englishman Dalton published a table that listed the elements classified according to their relative mass. The Swedish chemist Jöns Jakob Berzelius (1779–1848) refined Dalton's table of atomic masses and introduced an alphabetic system of abbreviations for the elements that are used to this day.

Investigations carried out in the 1800s suggested that certain elements have similar characteristics. One night, the Russian chemist Dmitri Mendelyev (1834–1907) cut out small cards with the names of all the known elements. He arranged them into a grid where elements with similar properties were arranged vertically. He called this grid 'the periodic table of the elements'. With some changes, this is the system that chemists use to this day. The modern periodic system consists of about a hundred elements, and there are no more to be found in nature.

Now, the quest continues to understand the internal composition of the atom.

Solids, liquids and gases

Investigation	Curriculum links

Classroom investigations

The ice balloon

to make the connection between freezing and melting

Sc1 2f: explore, using the senses of sight, hearing, smell, touch and taste as appropriate, and make and record observations and measurements

Sc3 2b: explore and describe the way some everyday materials change when they are heated or cooled

SIS B: use simple equipment and techniques to make observations and measurements

KUE B: describe how everyday materials can be changed by heating or cooling

KMC a: find out about the effect of heating and cooling some everyday substances, such as water, chocolate or butter

Ice and salt

to understand that a mixture of water and salt has a lower freezing point than water alone

Sc1 2f: explore, using the senses of sight, hearing, smell, touch and taste as appropriate, and make and record observations and measurements

Sc3 2b: explore and describe the way some everyday materials change when they are heated or cooled

SIS B: use simple equipment and techniques to make observations and measurements

KUE B: describe how everyday materials can be changed by heating or cooling

INC a: make observations using their senses

KMC a: find out about the effect of heating and cooling some everyday substances, such as water, chocolate or butter

Further investigations

How do you stop an ice cube melting?

Two plastic bottles

Facts about...
solids, liquids and gases

Substances have different boiling points

Not all substances become a gas at the same temperature. Most people know that water boils at 100°C. This is the temperature at which water becomes a gas. Alcohol boils at 79°C, and iron has a boiling point of 2890°C. Nitrogen boils at ⁻196°C and is a gas at room temperature.

Atoms in solids, liquids and gases

Here is an easy dramatisation you can perform to illustrate the movement and various phases exhibited by atoms. Use children to represent the atoms of a given substance. Draw a circle of chalk on the playground, or place a plastic hoop on the classroom floor. Ask as many children as will fit to stand inside the circle. They represent the substance in its solid state. The atoms are almost still. The children should stand close together.

Now let's warm things up! Ask the children to move around a bit more, then ask one child, and then another, to step outside the circle. The remaining children should stand slightly further apart, and keep moving around. The substance has melted and is in the liquid phase!

Now we'll raise the temperature yet again. The atoms are now knocking into each other all the time, and more of them get knocked out of the circle, until there are only two atoms left, moving around within the circle, keeping their distance from each other. The substance has boiled, and is now a gas!

Condensation

If the temperature of a gas is lowered, eventually the atoms will slow down and begin getting closer. The proper term for this is 'condensation'. The gas becomes a liquid, and, if the temperature sinks further, it will eventually reach the point at which the substance freezes, and becomes a solid.

Absolute zero

There is a minimum temperature past which it can get no colder. This is referred to as 'absolute zero'. At this temperature, there is no atomic movement.

Changing state

This diagram shows what is happening at each stage when a substance changes from one state to another.

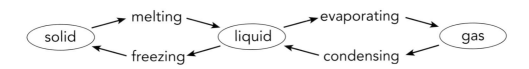

The three states of matter can also be demonstrated with corn!

The atoms are fixed in the same position.

The atoms move, but are only in contact with each other.

The atoms move in all directions.

COOKING WITH GAS

Jamie's step-dad is cooking dinner.

I wonder if it's the bubbles that cook the pasta...

PASTA

The pasta comes back up!

Look at this!

COIIO

It's sinking again! I've invented a magic pasta lift!

It's the gas bubbles that do it.

What's gas?

There are different kinds. You can sometimes see or smell them.

The water is boiling.

Where has all the water gone?

After dinner...

BURP!

Notes on the story

The pasta in the lemonade

As Meena says, gas lifts the pasta shell to the surface of the lemonade. The gas in the lemonade is less dense than the liquid. Gas bubbles attach themselves to the pasta, causing it to float. When it reaches the surface, the bubbles detach themselves from the pasta, and so it sinks back down. The name of the gas is carbon dioxide. When carbon dioxide is dissolved in water, it is referred to as carbonic acid.

Boiling water

We usually see water in its liquid state. When water boils, it changes from a liquid to a gas. The boiling point for water is 100°C. When water is boiling, its temperature cannot be raised further by turning up the temperature on the stove. This would add more energy – the water would boil more vigorously and the transition from liquid to gas would occur more quickly – but the temperature of the water will not change as long as it is boiling.

The ice balloon

 Fill the balloon with water. Tie a knot in it so the water cannot escape.

 Put the balloon in the freezer for a few days.

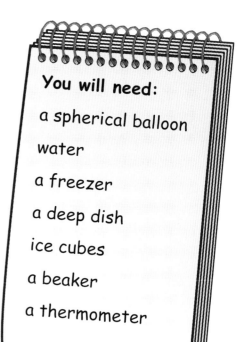

You will need:

a spherical balloon

water

a freezer

a deep dish

ice cubes

a beaker

a thermometer

How cold is it inside the freezer?

What do you think is going to happen to the balloon and the water? Draw and write about it.

 Remove the balloon from the freezer. Take the balloon off and throw it away. Put the contents on the dish and examine it.

How does it look? How does it feel?

What do you think will happen now?

 Put several ice cubes in the beaker. Use the thermometer to measure the temperature.

How many degrees does the thermometer show?

How do you think the temperature will change in half an hour?

 Measure the temperature of the ice every 5 minutes over the course of half an hour.

 Draw and write about your results.

The ice balloon

Learning objective: to make the connection between freezing and melting

Curriculum links

England/Wales:	Sc1 2f; Sc3 2b
Scotland:	SIS B; KUE B
Northern Ireland:	KMC a

Experiment summary

Children fill balloons with water and freeze them a couple of days before this lesson. Ask children to think about what might be happening to the water in the balloon. They should draw and write about their theories. The children take the balloons out of the freezer on the day of the lesson. They strip the balloons away and examine the ice. They describe how the ice looks and feels, and think about what will happen to the ice now that it is out of the freezer.

Then give the children some ice cubes (it is easier to measure the temperature of these than that of the ice balloon). Children put their ice cubes in a beaker and take the temperature at 5-minute intervals over the space of half an hour, recording their results.

Tips

Make sure children do not overfill the balloons.

Use alcohol thermometers or digital thermometers with a scale from ⁻15°C to ⁺150°C.

To save time, you could bring ready-frozen ice balloons to the lesson. Wrap them in newspaper to keep them cold. You could discuss this at the end of the lesson if you like: the newspaper traps air between its layers, which works as an insulator and helps to keep the temperature the same.

Expected results

The water in the balloon will freeze and become ice. If the block of ice is then left at room temperature, it will melt. This will take a long time, and will vary depending on the air temperature in the classroom.

The temperature of the ice cubes in the beaker will remain at a constant 0°C until all the ice has melted. Then it will rise until it reaches room temperature. Children often do not expect this.

Explanation

The freezing point of water is 0°C. Putting the water balloon in the freezer causes the atoms to become colder, making them slow down and move closer together until the liquid becomes a solid (ice). When the ice is exposed to a warmer air temperature, it starts to melt (it changes from a solid to a liquid). Water melts when the air temperature is more than 0°C. However, while the ice is melting, the temperature of the ice will stay at 0°C.

Everyday examples

Ask the children to think of other things they know of that can freeze or melt. Butter melts within a range of room temperatures. Iron requires the unbelievably high temperature of a foundry (1537°C) to melt. Chocolate, luckily, melts in your mouth!

Ice and salt

 1 Pull the balloon off the ice and put the block of ice in the dish.

 2 Sprinkle two tablespoons of salt on top of the ice.

You will need:
- a ready-made ice balloon
- a deep dish
- a tablespoon
- salt
- food colouring
- ice cubes
- a beaker
- a thermometer

What happens? Look and listen!

 3 Put a couple of drops of food colouring on the ice.

What happens? Draw and write about what you see.

 4 Pour lots of salt on the centre of the top of the ice. Leave it for half an hour.

How does it look after half an hour?

 5 Put some ice cubes into the beaker. Add two tablespoons of salt. Measure the temperature a few times over the next 10 minutes.

What are your results? Is this what you expected to happen?

 6 Put the dish with the block of ice on a windowsill. Leave it there for a few days.

What do you think will happen?

 7 Draw and write about the results.

Ice and salt

Learning objective: to understand that a mixture of water and salt has a lower freezing point than water alone

Curriculum links

England/Wales:	Sc1 2f; Sc3 2b
Scotland:	SIS B; KUE B
Northern Ireland:	INC a; KMC a

Everyday examples

In wintertime, roads are salted in order to prevent accidents. A salt solution needs a lower temperature to freeze than plain water, and so adding salt prevents ice from forming. The grit helps to break up any ice which has already formed.

People used to make ice-cream by mixing salt with ice to achieve a very low temperature.

Further ideas

The ice balloon stirs the minds of most children. Here are some examples of the questions that may crop up and how you can respond: Does the mass of the balloon change after it has been in the freezer? (Try weighing before and after. The mass does not change.) Does the size of the balloon change after it has been in the freezer? (Measure the circumference with a measuring tape before and after. The size increases.) Does the ice balloon float? (Test in a tub of water. The ice balloon floats.)

Experiment summary

Prepare some ice balloons in advance (fill balloons with water, tie the necks and put them in a freezer for a few days). Each group of children takes their ice block out of the balloon and puts it on a dish. First, they sprinkle salt on the ice. Next, they put some food colouring on the ice. Then, they pour lots more salt on and leave the ice for half an hour. At each stage, they observe and describe what happens. Then, they put some ice cubes in a beaker and add salt. They use a thermometer to measure the temperature a few times over a 10-minute period. They discuss the results. Lastly, they put their ice block on a windowsill (still in its dish!) and leave it for a couple of days. They discuss the results.

Expected results

Sometimes you will hear a crackling sound when you pour salt on ice. Cracks may also form. When the food colouring is added, it will sink into the melting ice in a pretty, branching pattern. When the ice balloon has sat for half an hour with salt on it, there will be a large hole in the middle. The salt in the beaker of ice will cause the temperature to fall to 17–18 degrees below zero. Without the salt, it would remain at around 0°C until the ice melted. Once the block of ice on the windowsill has melted and the water has evaporated, only the salt and food colouring will remain. The salt will have formed crystals.

Explanation

Salt is made up of ions. An ion is an atom that has taken on or lent out electrons, and therefore carries a charge. The ions are arranged into large crystals. When the salt comes into contact with the ice, the salt crystals are broken into smaller pieces which dissolve in the water molecules on the surface of the ice block. Energy is required in order to break the bonds that hold the salt crystals together. This energy is taken from the water, which causes the temperature of the solution to fall. The salt lowers the temperature of the surface of the ice, but the temperature inside remains the same. This creates a tension which is what causes the crackling sound. The food colouring helps us to see more clearly how the ice balloon has melted.

Further investigations

How do you stop an ice cube melting?

You will need: ice cubes; lots of different materials for insulation

Experiment

Ask the children to think about how they could stop an ice cube melting. They may not use a freezer, refrigerator or other ice cubes! Make sure they have all the equipment they need, then allow them to begin their experiments. Remind them to take careful measurements, using a stop watch to time from when they take their ice cube from the freezer and wrap it up.

Tips

You will need to make sure that there are plenty of materials around the classroom for the children to use to test their theories. Try to think of all the materials they might suggest: fabric, polystyrene, sawdust, newspaper, cardboard, tissue paper, aluminium foil, plastic bags, and so on.

Expected results

Children will have a variety of suggestions about what materials might keep the ice cube from melting. Successful insulating materials might be polystyrene, wool, newspaper, light-coloured or reflective materials, bubble wrap. The children may also think about where they place their ice cube. It will be colder by the floor than by the ceiling, and it would be sensible to keep the ice cubes away from items such as lamps that generate heat!

Explanation

Energy naturally transfers from warmer objects or areas to cooler ones. The idea is to reduce this transfer so that the ice remains cold. Fluffy fabric and newspaper are good insulators because a lot of air can be trapped in them; air is a poor conductor of heat. White or shiny materials reflect the radiated heat away from the ice cube. It is colder by the floor than by the ceiling because warm air rises.

Two plastic bottles

You will need: two plastic bottles with caps; water

Experiment

Fill one of the bottles right to the top with water. Leave the other one full of air. Put the cap tightly on each bottle. Pass both bottles around the class. Children squeeze the bottles and describe how they feel.

Expected results

The bottle containing air can be partly compressed, but the one containing water cannot.

Explanation

The 'empty' bottle is filled with air, which is a gas. In a gas, the molecules are spread out widely. When the bottle is squeezed, we see an important property of gases that differentiates them from solids and liquids: gases are easy to compress. When you squeeze the bottle, you are forcing the molecules closer to one another. This is not possible with water.

A short history of...
solids, liquids and gases

Fire

A big leap in the progress of civilisation occurred when humans learned to use fire. Palaeontologists have found fire rings that are 600 000 years old. Fire gives heat and light. The fire ring became a meeting place, and to this day we feel something special when we gather around a camp fire. We are able to explain that the flames are gases and that the coals are burning solids, and we can name the precise boiling point of water, and we know that the bubbles that form are steam. Yet fire nevertheless exerts a mystical charm over us.

Ancient ideas about evaporation and condensation

The Greek philosophers conducted experiments and began to form ideas about the nature of evaporation and condensation. For instance, they thought that the steam formed by boiling water was air, and that dew was air turned into water. The fact that a residue of salt and dirt is left behind when water evaporates was accounted for as earth. Earth, air, fire and water were the four elements thought to comprise the building blocks of all matter.

Hero's use of steam

Hero, a Greek mathematician and inventor from Alexandria in the first century AD, made a device for opening temple gates. He used boiling water to create enough force to pull open the gates. The fire was placed on an altar, beneath which was a vessel of water. Hero made use of the fact that that pressure increases as water rises in temperature. Hero also invented a 'steam engine ball'. This was a ball filled with water with pipes set at angles. It is not known whether Hero succeeded in making his ball spin, but in principle it was a simple steam turbine. How amazing that the ancient Greeks were so near to inventing a functional steam turbine! It was not until the 1600s that James Watt constructed his first steam engine.

History of gas

The word 'gas' was coined by the Belgian Jan Baptist van Helmont (1577–1644). He was the first person to realise that there are many different gases with different properties. The Swede Carl Wilhelm von Scheele (1742–1786) managed to produce pure oxygen, and also investigated another gas found in the atmosphere. He found that four-fifths of air is not used in combustion, and referred to this useless part as 'corrupted air'. The gas he found was nitrogen. It was only in the 1700s, with chemists like Lavoisier, that science hit upon the thought that most substances could be found as solids, liquids and gases.

Mercury

Mercury is an unusual metal that is a liquid at room temperature. These days it is used in thermometers because it expands when the temperature rises. It used to be used for a much more dangerous job though: extracting gold from river silt. People used to pour mercury (or quicksilver, as it used to be called) into the pan, where it would become bound to the small grains of gold. This process is called amalgamation. The lumps of amalgam were then sifted out and heated until the mercury evaporated, leaving pure gold. The process was dangerous because mercury is a 'heavy metal' that can lead to neurological or genetic damage if its fumes are inhaled.

Solutions and suspensions

 Investigation

Curriculum links

Classroom investigations

The sugar cube
to observe the creation of a solution

Sc1 2i: compare what happened with what they expected would happen, and try to explain it, drawing on their knowledge and understanding
KS2 Sc3 3b: that some solids dissolve in water to give solutions but some do not
KUE B: give examples of everyday materials that dissolve in water
INI d: relate what happened to what they predicted
KMC b: investigate which everyday substances dissolve in water

Test the sugar
to see if different types of sugar cube dissolve differently

Sc1 2i: compare what happened with what they expected would happen, and try to explain it, drawing on their knowledge and understanding
KS2 Sc3 3b: that some solids dissolve in water to give solutions but some do not
KUE B: give examples of everyday materials that dissolve in water
INI d: relate what happened to what they predicted
KMC b: investigate which everyday substances dissolve in water

Home investigations

Sugar and water

Further investigations

The chemical garden

Facts about...
solutions and suspensions

A mixture of substances

In nature, substances get mixed with each other all the time. When substances are mixed, the mixture gains new properties. Humans have made use of this fact throughout the ages. Just think about cooking and how good things can taste if we use exactly the right recipe.

Solutions and suspensions are both 'mixtures'. In science, a mixture is two or more substances that can be separated again because their molecules have not been changed chemically. A solution is a mixture that has the same properties throughout (for example, a solution of water and sugar, which will taste equally sugary throughout). A suspension is a mixture in which fine grains can be separated out (for example, biscuit crumbs in a cup of tea). The substances in a suspension can often by separated fairly simply by a method such as filtering. The substances in a solution are more difficult to separate, but it can be done by methods such as evaporating the liquid to leave the solid behind.

Sugar and water

Water is an excellent solvent. Many substances will dissolve in it. You know what happens when you put a sugar cube in water: first you see the sugar cube, then after a while it seems to have disappeared. If you taste the water, you'll know the sugar is still there, yet you cannot tell what is water and what is sugar. This is what is called a solution.

Like all matter, sugar is made up of atoms. In sugar, several atoms have combined to form molecules. When you put a sugar cube in water, the water molecules will tear the sugar molecules off the cube and carry them away throughout the contents of the container. The sugar will dissolve more quickly if the water is heated, because the water molecules move faster when they are warmer. The sugar will also dissolve more quickly if it is ground into smaller pieces, because more of the sugar is in contact with the water. You cannot separate the water from the sugar even by pouring the solution through a filter. The molecules are much smaller than the holes in the paper, and they easily pass through with the water.

The difference between melting and dissolving

In chemistry, melting and dissolving are different things. A substance melts when it changes from a solid to a liquid state, for example when you melt sugar in a saucepan it becomes a liquid. To dissolve, a substance must be mixed with a liquid.

Everyday examples of solutions and suspensions

To make bronze, copper and tin are melted so they are both liquids. The two substances are then mixed together, and they become a solution. When they are left to cool, they become a solid again, and it looks like just one substance.

To make glue, plastic is dissolved in a solvent, so it is liquid when it is in the tube or pot. When the glue is applied, it is exposed to the air. This makes the solvent evaporate, which leaves just the plastic, which holds the glued surfaces together.

WHAT'S THE SOLUTION?

Notes on the story

The salt in the juice

Salt dissolves in liquid. When Jamie puts salt in his juice, the salt molecules have become joined to the water molecules, so Jamie can taste both juice and salt when he eats the toast he has dipped in the mixture. All of the juice tastes of salt, because the salt is mixed all the way through it. This is a solution. When Jamie stirs the juice with a spoon, he helps the salt to dissolve more quickly.

The toast in the juice

When Jamie dips his toast into the juice, crumbs of the toast fall into the glass and get mixed into the juice when Jamie stirs them. The toast does not dissolve, though. The toast and juice do not become a solution. The toast crumbs are in the juice, but Jamie can see them, and they can be removed from the juice with some effort. This is a suspension.

The coffee filter

Jamie decides to try filtering the juice. This works for the toast crumbs – these are much larger than the tiny holes in the filter paper, and so the juice would pass through and the toast crumbs would be trapped on top. This works because the toast crumbs are only suspended in the juice. The filter does not work for the salt. When the salt dissolves into the juice, molecules of water and salt are formed. These molecules are much smaller than the holes in the filter paper, and so they easily pass through the filter.

Looking for a solution

Jamie looks all round the kitchen for something that might separate the salt from the juice. The refrigerator would not help him; it would only make the solution colder. The freezer wouldn't help; it would freeze the entire contents of his glass. The oven wouldn't help either; the heat would make the water evaporate, and all Jamie would have left in the glass would be a burned mixture of toast crumbs, salt and the sugar from the juice.

The sugar cube

You will need:

a transparent beaker

warm water

a sugar cube

 1 Fill the beaker with warm water.

What do you think will happen if you put a sugar cube in the water?

 2 Draw and describe what you think will happen.

 3 Put the sugar cube in the beaker. Don't stir the water!

What happens? Is it what you expected?

 4 Draw and describe what happened.

How does the water taste?

The sugar cube

Learning objective: to observe the creation of a solution

Curriculum links

England/Wales:	Sc1 2i;
	KS2 Sc3 3b
Scotland:	KUE B
Northern Ireland:	INI d; KMC b

Make sure the beakers are thoroughly clean and that the water is safe to drink.

Investigation summary

Ask children to think about what will happen when a sugar cube is placed in warm water. Children then try the investigation, and draw and describe what happens. They then taste the water.

Expected results

It will look as if the sugar cube is being 'eaten' by the water, or that it is 'melting' or 'withering away'. After a while, the sugar cube will disappear completely, but a taste test will reveal that the whole beaker of water is sweet.

Explanation

A sugar cube is made up of small crystals. These are visible to the eye. The crystals, in turn, are made up of many sugar molecules. They are far too small for the eye to be able to see them individually. The water is made up of water molecules. These water molecules are in constant motion, because it is a liquid. When we put the sugar in the water, the water molecules tear sugar molecules away from the outside of the sugar cube, pull them into solution, and spread them throughout the beaker. Once the sugar cube has 'disappeared', the water molecules and sugar molecules have blended, and are found in the same proportions throughout the beaker. This is why you can taste water from anywhere in the beaker with no difference in sweetness.

Everyday example

Many products found in the home are solutions: glue, liquid soap, shampoo, washing-up liquid, fruit drinks, soup stock and much more.

Further ideas

An alternative demonstration is to put some sugar cubes in a transparent jug on the overhead projector. This shows clearly how the sugar dissolves and spreads throughout the water. It looks as though the sugar is radiating off the cube.

Test the sugar

 Plan an investigation to find out which type of sugar cube dissolves the fastest in water.

How are you going to conduct your test?

What do you think the results will be?

You will need:

two or more types of sugar cube

two or more beakers

warm water

 Carry out your investigation!

 Draw and describe what you did.

 Draw and describe your results.

Did it turn out the way you predicted?

Test the sugar

Learning objective: to see if different types of sugar cube dissolve differently

Curriculum links

England/Wales: Sc1 2i;

KS2 Sc3 3b

Scotland: KUE B

Northern Ireland: INI d; KMC b

Further ideas

This investigation can also be conducted as a demonstrative investigation with two transparent bowls on the overhead projector. Ask the children to write down or tell you their hypotheses.

You could also conduct 'the toffee test': you can demonstrate that identical toffees can be made to dissolve at different rates. You will need three identical toffees. Ask for three volunteers. The first child holds a toffee in their mouth without chewing or sucking. The second child doesn't chew the toffee, but moves it around in their mouth. The third chews the toffee *and* moves it around in their mouth. If you do not want to encourage the children to eat sweets during lessons, you can always volunteer your own services to science and act as a guinea pig!

Investigation summary

Give each group of children two or more different types of sugar cube (preferably all the same size), the same number of beakers as sugar cubes, and a jug of warm water (water from the hot tap is fine). Set children the challenge of planning and conducting an investigation to see which type of sugar cube dissolves the fastest. Encourage them to consider at each stage of their investigation whether their test is fair.

Expected results

There are different types of sugar that dissolve at different rates. The fastest to dissolve will probably be the type whose name indicates as much!

In order to perform the test correctly, it is a good idea to start with a list summarising 'things that can change' (variables). In this case, the variables might be the type of sugar cube, the size of the glass, the volume of the water, the water temperature, and how much the solution is stirred. To test for the type of sugar that dissolves the fastest, nothing should be changed except for the type of sugar. The children should use identical beakers with the same volume of water; the water must be at the same temperature; the sugar cubes must be of a single size; and the water should not be stirred at all. This adds up to a fair test.

Explanation

The rate at which the sugar dissolves in water depends on the size of the crystals that make up the sugar cube, and this in turn depends on the strength of the crystals' bonds to each other. We can't tell just by looking at two sugar cubes which one will dissolve faster; we have to conduct a test.

Home investigation

Sugar and water

 Fill one beaker with warm water.

 Fill the other beaker with cold water.

 Put the ice cube in the cold water.

 Put one sugar cube in each beaker.

What happens to the sugar cubes?

What happens to the ice cube?

What happens to the water?

 Draw and describe what happened.

You will need:
two beakers
warm water
cold water
an ice cube
two sugar cubes

96

Home investigation teacher notes

Sugar and water

Investigation summary

Each child has one beaker of warm water and one beaker of cold water. They put an ice cube in the cold water, and then put one sugar cube into each beaker. They observe what happens to the sugar cubes, the ice cube, and the water (they will have to taste the water to find out what has happened to it).

Expected results

Both sugar cubes will dissolve, but the one in the warm water will dissolve faster. The ice cube will melt. The water in both beakers will taste sweet.

Explanation

As we know from earlier investigations in this chapter, when a sugar cube is placed in water, the water, which is in constant motion, tears sugar molecules away from the outside of the sugar cube, pulling them into solution and spreading them throughout the beaker. The molecules in warm water move faster, and so the sugar molecules will blend with the water molecules faster in warm water than in cold.

The ice undergoes a state change from solid to liquid.

Further investigations

The chemical garden

You will need: gelatine powder; a beaker; sugar cubes; food colouring; instant coffee; tea leaves; tweezers

Investigation

Perform this investigation as a demonstration. Before the lesson, follow the instructions on the gelatine packet and make up some gelatine in the beaker. Colour parts of sugar cubes with food colouring. Once the gelatine has set (this will take about a day), push the sugar cubes, coffee granules and tea leaves down into the gelatine using the tweezers. Leave the beaker for a week, then see what has happened to it.

Expected results

Coloured branches and wreaths will grow out from the sugar cubes, coffee granules and tea leaves.

Explanation

The various colouring agents dissolve in the water–gelatine solution, and the molecules of the solution have been spreading away from the objects. The gelatine makes the water very thick and jelly-like, which means the molecules move around much, much more slowly than in plain water. Therefore the molecules of the water–gelatine–colouring solution will spread very slowly throughout the gelatine, which is why the contents of the beaker will not be entirely blended after a week.

A short history of...
solutions and suspensions

Salt as a solution

We get most of our salt from sea water. We all know that sea water tastes salty! It is a solution, and we have to separate the salt from the water. The most common method of doing this is to put the sea water in large basins. The water evaporates, leaving the salt behind. Salt is also found deep in the earth. This salt can be extracted by pumping hot water into the ground, which dissolves the salt. This solution can then be brought to the surface, where the water can be evaporated.

Salt was one of man's most important early commodities. Roman soldiers were sometimes paid in salt, and this is where the word 'salary' comes from: 'sal' is Latin for 'salt'. Salt was used as a preservative, which solved the problem of storing food during the winter. It is necessary that our diets contain enough salt for our bodies to function.

Water as a solvent

When humans began settling in cities, much inventiveness was required to make sure that the people had access to clean drinking water. Water is a very good solvent, which means that other substances easily become dissolved in it. Problems arise when bacteria get mixed in with drinking water, which can lead to disease. The large cities of the 1800s were notoriously unhealthy. It was only towards the end of the 1800s that water filtering systems were put into use to cleanse the water for drinking.

Colour solutions

Around 5000 years ago, Egyptian potters experimented with mixing different coloured substances to make coloured solutions. They used these to glaze their pottery.

99

Investigation

Curriculum links

Classroom investigations

Two magnets

to understand that magnets have two poles that attract or repel each other

Sc4 2b: that both pushes and pulls are examples of forces

KS2 Sc4 2a: about the forces of attraction and repulsion between magnets, and about the forces of attraction between magnets and magnetic materials

KUF B: describe the interaction of magnets in terms of the forces of attraction and repulsion

KPF a: explore forces which push, pull or make things move

Is it magnetic?

to understand that some things are attracted to a magnet while others are not

Sc4 2b: that both pushes and pulls are examples of forces

KS2 Sc4 2a: about the forces of attraction and repulsion between magnets, and about the forces of attraction between magnets and magnetic materials

KUF B: describe the interaction of magnets in terms of the forces of attraction and repulsion

KPF a: explore forces which push, pull or make things move

Home investigations

The strongest magnet

Further investigations

Magnet games

Facts about...

Magnets and metals

Magnetism is an invisible, sometimes seemingly magical, force. Magnets are objects that attract metal. Magnets can be made from iron, nickel, copper, cobalt and even ceramic (ceramic magnets are called magnadur magnets). Magnets do not attract all metals. They attract iron, nickel and cobalt. The fact that not all metals are attracted by magnets comes in very handy for helping us to decide which metal food and drink cans can be recycled. Cans are usually made of steel or aluminium. Although both steel and aluminium can be recycled, steel cans have a thin coating of tin which needs to be removed before the steel can be used again. You can find out very quickly whether a can is made of aluminium or steel by holding a magnet to the side. Steel is magnetic because it is made with iron, so if the magnet is attracted, the can is steel!

Permanent and natural magnets

In schools, we would usually use 'permanent' magnets. These are made of special metals that can be strongly magnetised and retain their magnetic properties for a long time. But there are also 'natural magnets', or 'lodestones'. These are rocks, and although we might not think that a rock could be a magnet, they contain a lot of iron.

Magnetic north

One very useful property of magnets is that if you hang one up and leave it to swing freely, one end of it will point towards north. We call the direction in which a magnet points 'magnetic north'. A compass is made by fixing a magnet inside a case so it can swing round freely. Since it will always point towards north, it can help you to find the right direction if you get lost.

Cow magnets

In some countries, such as the USA, farmers will sometimes make their cows swallow a magnet. Cows do not always notice what they are eating along with grass, and they often eat metal objects such as nails or barbed wire. These can be very harmful if they go too far through the cow's digestive system. The magnet will stay in the cow's first stomach (remember, a cow has four stomachs!), and all the bits of metal it eats will be attracted to the magnet and stay there with it.

A FATAL ATTRACTION

Notes on the story

The fridge magnet

Lots of people put magnets on their refrigerators. The doors are made out of a metal that contains iron. Iron is one of the metals that are attracted to magnets. This is what holds the magnet to the fridge door. Some people use this force to hold photos or notes to the door.

The paper clip

Paper clips are usually made of iron, and so they are attracted to the magnet. The magnetic force is strong enough to attract the paper clip even through the glass. Jamie is able to slide the paper clip all the way to the top of the glass, which allows him to get it out without touching the paper clip or the water.

 Two magnets

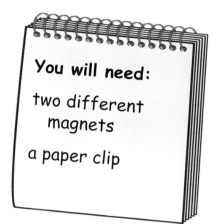
You will need:
two different magnets
a paper clip

 Hold the two magnets together.

What happens?

 Try turning one of the magnets around and holding a different part of it next to the other magnet.

What happens?

 Try the same tests, but put a sheet of paper between the two magnets.

Do the same things happen?

 Try the same tests, but hold one magnet on the top of a desk, and the other magnet underneath the desk.

Do the same things happen?

 Try to pick the paper clip up from the desk by using different parts of each magnet.

Which parts have the strongest attraction?

 Think about how you could test to see which of the two magnets is stronger.

Two magnets

Learning objective: to understand that magnets have two poles that attract or repel each other

Curriculum links

England/Wales:	Sc4 2b;
	KS2 Sc4 2a
Scotland:	KUF B
Northern Ireland:	KPF a

Magnets can damage televisions, computer screens, computer disks and clocks.

Everyday examples

There are various types of magnet to be found around the home, for example fridge magnets, magnetic knife holders, cupboard door latches and parts of toys. The magnetic strip that holds a refrigerator door closed is a safety feature to stop children getting locked inside! The magnet allows the door to be pushed open from the inside. Other clever uses of magnets are magnetic screwdrivers that hold the screw for you, and the torches that you can 'hang up' with a magnet.

Investigation summary

Each group of children needs two different magnets (for example, bar, horseshoe, button). Children investigate what happens when they hold different ends or parts of the magnets together. They then test to see if the magnets behave in the same way when there is a piece of paper or a desk top between them. Next, they use a paper clip to test which part of each magnet attracts the paper clip most strongly. Finally, they think about how they could test to find out which of the two magnets has the stronger force.

Expected results

Different parts of the magnets attract and repel each other. You can make magnets jump, dance and slide by holding them together in different ways. The magnetic force will penetrate paper, and should even penetrate a desk top. Both the thickness of the desk top and the strength of the magnet will affect the results. Children should be aware, however, that magnetic force does have limits. The part of the magnet that exerts the most force depends on its shape, but for most magnets the force is stronger at the ends than in middle. Which magnet is stronger will depend on what types of magnet the children are using.

Explanation

There is no very simple way to explain why two magnets attract and repel each other in particular ways. You can explain to the children that one end points north and the other points south, and that we call these the magnet's north and south poles. If you place a north pole and a south pole together, they will be attracted to each other and 'pull together'. If you place two south poles or two north poles together, they will be repelled from each other, and jump apart.

Is it magnetic?

You will need:

a magnet

a container of various small objects

Which of the objects in the container do you think will *be* attracted to the magnet?

Try it! Put the magnet in the container, move it around so it touches all the objects, and then take it out.

Which *objects* are held by the magnet? Were you right?

Draw a table and write down things which were attracted and things which weren't.

Do the things that were attracted have anything in common?

Is it magnetic?

Learning objective: to understand that some things are attracted to a magnet while others are not

Curriculum links

England/Wales:	Sc4 2b;
	KS2 Sc4 2a
Scotland:	KUF B
Northern Ireland:	KPF a

Everyday examples

One way we use magnetism on a daily basis is on credit cards. If you are able to pour iron filings along the dark strip on the back, a pattern will emerge (a series of horizontal stripes not unlike a barcode). This will show how we use magnetism to store information. Examples of the same technique, albeit containing much more information, are video cassettes, floppy disks, anti-theft devices and magnetic locks.

Further ideas

Iron filings are ideal for demonstrating magnetic properties. Put some in a flat, transparent container (it must be larger than the magnet). Place a bar magnet on an overhead projector. Place the container of iron filings on top of the magnet. The filings will arrange themselves into a beautiful picture of how the magnetic field radiates out from each of the poles.

Investigation summary

Give each group of children a magnet (bar magnets work well for this) and a pot or tub containing around 10 small objects, some magnetic and some not, for example an iron screw, a brass screw, aluminium foil, a rubber band, a stone, a piece of magnetite (if you can find one), a small pencil stub, a paper clip, a staple, a piece of magnetic tape, and so on. Children predict which of the objects will be attracted to the magnet. They then test to see if they were right by moving the magnet around the objects to see which ones are pulled towards it. Children record their findings in a simple table.

Expected results

When the children take the magnet out of the tub, some of the objects will be attached to the magnet. These will be the objects that are made out of iron, nickel or cobalt, the magnetite (if you managed to get some), and the magnetic tape, which is coated with a layer of iron.

Explanation

Only three metals have magnetic properties: iron, nickel and cobalt. There is no simple explanation of the magnetic properties of iron, so if the children really want to know why iron is magnetic, you may have to resort to the atomic model. All matter consists of atoms. One of the parts of the atom is the electron, which is a particle which carries a negative charge. An iron atom contains many electrons that revolve around the core (nucleus) of the atom. It just so happens that in an iron atom many of the electrons are revolving in the same direction. This is what creates the magnetic properties. When the electrons move, a magnetic field is created.

Home investigation

The strongest magnet

You will need:

two or more magnets

| Which magnet do you think will be the strongest? |

 Think about how you could test the magnets to find out.

 Plan your test.

What do you think the results will be?

 Carry out your test.

 Describe your test and what happened.

Were you right?

Home investigation teacher notes

The strongest magnet

Investigation summary

Children devise a test to find out which of two or more magnets is the strongest. They make a prediction about what will happen. They conduct their evaluation, and then describe the results.

Expected results

Children might come up with tests such as finding out how many paper clips each magnet can hold in a chain, or how close a paper clip has to be to be pulled towards the magnet. The results of their investigations will depend on what magnets were available at home for them to use. Sometimes the smallest magnet is the strongest, so children may be surprised by their results!

Explanation

Horseshoe magnets are stronger than bar magnets of the same size and material because the magnetic poles are closer together. The magnetic strength from one pole to the other is greatly increased because the magnetic field is concentrated in a smaller area.

Further investigations

Magnet games

You will need: paper clips; a wooden or plastic tray; a magnet; a glass, a saucepan lid or a jar lid

Investigation

Ask children to carry out these three investigations:

a) Pour some paper clips onto the wooden or plastic tray. Place the magnet against the bottom of the tray and move it around. What happens?

b) Build a chain of paper clips hanging from the magnet. How long can you make it? What happens if you remove the paper clip that is closest to the magnet?

c) Can a magnetic force penetrate a glass, a saucepan lid or the lid of a jar? Use the magnet and paper clips to investigate.

Expected results

a) The paper clips will follow the movement of the magnet. You can make them 'dance'!

b) The length of the chain will depend on the strength of the magnet. If you remove the paper clip closest to the magnet, the chain will be broken and the other paper clips will fall down. If the magnet is very strong, the second paper clip in the chain may be pulled upwards towards the magnet.

c) A magnetic force will penetrate glass and aluminium because these materials are not magnetic. When you try it with the jar lid, paper clips will be attracted to the edges of the lid, but not very strongly.

Explanation

Paper clips are attracted to magnets because the magnet aligns all the tiny 'atom magnets' in the same direction, but only as long as the magnet is nearby. A jar lid will shield the magnetic force because the whole lid becomes a magnet. The paper clips will be only weakly attracted to the edges of the lid because the magnetic force is spread across the whole of the jar lid, dissipating its strength.

Further ideas
You can show the children how to magnetise a paper clip by stroking one with a magnet 30 or so times in the same direction.

A short history of...
magnets

Magnetic rock
About 2500 years ago, according to legend, a Greek shepherd was guiding his flock to Mount Ida in Magnesia, Turkey. He suddenly found it hard to move his feet. The iron nails of his sandals held fast to the rock beneath them, and the iron tip of his crook was pulled towards the boulders all around. The shepherd had stumbled across lodestone, or magnetite, and discovered the strange power of magnetism.

Gilbert's magnetic sphere
In the year 1600, the English doctor William Gilbert (1540–1603) published a book called 'On the magnet'. He deduced that the earth was one giant magnet. He came up with a hypothesis about how a compass would behave in places such as the North and South Poles, based on his observation that the magnetic axis was very similar in position to the earth's axis. His method of testing his theory was to create a model of the earth: a magnetised sphere, which he called a 'terrella'. He then passed a compass around it, which showed that the needle always pointed north–south, and dipped towards the earth's axis.
Gilbert also described how to make a magnet by heating and beating a piece of iron and then letting it cool whilst oriented in a north–south direction.

Early compasses
By the 12th century, the Chinese had discovered that a hanging piece of magnetite would point in a north–south direction. A hundred years later, compasses were being used in Europe.

Electromagnetism
In 1820, Hans Christian Örstedt (1777–1851), a Danish scientist, discovered by accident that when a compass was placed near a source of electricity, the compass needle changed direction. In 1831, the English physicist Michael Faraday (1791–1867) succeeded in proving that electricity can be generated with the aid of a magnet. A German company called Siemens developed Faraday's ideas and started to manufacture generators. It was now possible to 'manufacture' electricity and soon there were electric lights in every home.

Air

Investigation	Curriculum links
Classroom investigations	
The paper in the glass *to understand that air takes up space*	Sc1 2b: use first-hand experience and simple information sources to answer questions Sc1 2i: compare what happened with what they expected would happen, and try to explain it, drawing on their knowledge and understanding SIS B: answer questions on the meaning of the findings INI a: talk to the teacher and others about what happened or about what they have made INI d: relate what happened to what they predicted
The empty bottle *to understand that air takes up space*	Sc1 2b: use first-hand experience and simple information sources to answer questions Sc1 2i: compare what happened with what they expected would happen, and try to explain it, drawing on their knowledge and understanding SIS B: answer questions on the meaning of the findings INI a: talk to the teacher and others about what happened or about what they have made INI d: relate what happened to what they predicted
Dropping paper *to understand that air offers resistance*	KS2 Sc4 2c: about friction, including air resistance, as a force that slows moving objects and may prevent objects from starting to move KUE C: describe air resistance in terms of friction KS2 KPF c: investigate how forces can affect the movement and shape of objects
The air cannon *to feel air in motion; to see the effect of a pressure wave*	KS2 Sc4 2c: about friction, including air resistance, as a force that slows moving objects and may prevent objects from starting to move KUE C: describe air resistance in terms of friction KS2 KPF c: investigate how forces can affect the movement and shape of objects
Balancing balloons *to understand that air has mass*	Sc1 2b: use first-hand experience and simple information sources to answer questions Sc1 2i: compare what happened with what they expected would happen, and try to explain it, drawing on their knowledge and understanding SIS B: answer questions on the meaning of the findings INI d: relate what happened to what they predicted
Home investigations	
The bag and the books	
Further investigations	
A stick under a newspaper	

Facts about...

What is air made of?

The air that we breathe is vital for us to exist. Air consists of nitrogen (around 78%), oxygen (around 21%) and a number of other gases (around 1%). An adult breathes in around 350 litres of air every day. We generally don't think of air as having mass, but 1 litre of air actually has a mass of around 1.3 grams!

Air resistance

If you run or cycle very quickly, you can feel the pressure of the air on your face – it feels like a breeze is blowing towards you. When something moves through the air, the air pushes back. Imagine you are trying to run into a brick wall. You wouldn't be able to move at all, would you? We can't move through a solid object. Now imagine you are running through water. You can move through water, but not as fast as you could move normally. The molecules in water move around much more freely than those in a solid object, so we can push them aside and pass through them. The molecules in air can move around very freely. When we move through air, we are still pushing molecules aside, but we can't usually feel it. This is called air resistance. The faster you try to move, the more air resistance you will feel. This is because when you move faster, you are trying to push more air out of the way, and the air pushes back more.

Changing air resistance

The amount of air resistance can also be changed by the shape of the object that is trying to move through it. If a javelin is thrown through the air, there will be very little air resistance. This is because the javelin will not need to push much air aside. If you held a large, flat sheet of cardboard in front of you and tried to run, you would find that you couldn't run as quickly as normal. This is because a large, flat object needs to push a lot of air aside to move through it, and so the air resistance is much greater. Sports cars have low, slanted bodies, to reduce the air resistance and allow them to move faster. The large, flat area of a parachute creates so much air resistance that it makes the parachute drop slowly enough to allow a person to fall thousands of metres without being harmed.

AN AIRY DAY

Jamie and Meena are on a bike ride.

The air is making your flag flap!

It's the speed that makes it flap, not air!

Air is nothing. You can't grab hold of it!

Air is all around us. We just can't see it.

Jamie pumps up his tyre.

A plane flies overhead.

If they used ordinary paint for planes, the air would wear it off.

Rubbish! Air can't do that.

Notes on the story

Jamie's tyre

The space inside a tyre is filled with air. Jamie's tyre has deflated a bit, so he uses a pump to put more air inside so it is completely filled.

Meena's flag

It's the air that makes the flag on Meena's bicycle flap. Although we can't see air, we can see its effects when things travel through it at speed.

The aeroplane

Air offers resistance when things move quickly through it, as we have already seen from the flag. An aeroplane flies incredibly fast. Concorde could fly at speeds of well over 1000 mph. Compare this to the speed at which you can cycle (about 10–15 mph). The air resistance when a plane is flying is so great that ordinary paint on the wings would be worn off!

The paper in the glass

 1 Half-fill the jug with water.

 2 Scrunch the piece of paper into a ball.
Push it to the bottom of the beaker.
Turn the beaker upside down.
Check that the paper doesn't fall out!

What do you think will happen to the paper if you put the upside-down beaker into the jug of water?

 3 Try it! Make sure you don't tip the beaker when you lower it into the water.

What happened? Were you right?

 4 Remove the paper from the beaker.
Place a matchstick on the surface of the water in the jug. Make sure it floats!

 5 Place the upside-down beaker over the matchstick.

 6 Look at the surface of the water inside the beaker and draw what it looks like.

Why do you think it looks like this?

Imagine you are the matchstick, and the beaker and jug are much larger! What do you think it would be like inside the beaker?

116

The paper in the glass

Learning objective: to understand that air takes up space

Curriculum links

England/Wales: Sc1 2b, 2i

Scotland: SIS B

Northern Ireland: INI a, d

Make sure you use spent matchsticks.

Investigation summary

Children push a ball of paper to the bottom of a transparent beaker and make sure it doesn't fall out when the beaker is turned over. They then put the upside-down beaker into a half-full jug of water, and observe what happens.

Then, children take the paper out of the beaker, and float a matchstick on the surface of the water in the jug. They then place the upside-down beaker over the top of the matchstick, and observe what the surface of the water inside the beaker looks like. They imagine what it would be like to be inside the beaker.

Tips

Make sure the jugs are not overfilled. Children should be able to place the upside-down beaker inside the jug without the jug overflowing. You could put newspaper underneath the jugs just in case!

Expected results

When the upside-down glass is placed in the water, the paper will not get wet, because the water will not rise up in the glass. This effect will be even more apparent when the children place the glass over the matchstick. The surface of the water inside the beaker will be much lower than that in the rest of the jug.

Explanation

Although it might look as though the beaker is empty, it is actually full of air. When it is placed in the water, the air in it cannot simply disappear! The water traps the air in, and so the water level cannot rise because the air is taking up that space.

Further ideas

Discuss the children's thoughts about how it would feel to be the matchstick. Explain that it is actually possible to go underwater in a huge 'glass'. Show a picture of a diving bell. This is an ancient invention that was used to salvage treasure from shipwrecks as early as the 17th century.

The empty bottle

 Insert the funnel into the neck of the bottle.
Seal around it with Blu-tack.

You will need:
a small funnel
a plastic bottle
Blu-tack
a small jug of water

What do you think will happen if you pour water into the funnel?

 Very slowly and steadily pour water into the funnel. Keep the bottle still!

What happened? Why do you think this happened?

The empty bottle

Learning objective: to understand that air takes up space

Curriculum links

England/Wales:	Sc1 2b, 2i
Scotland:	SIS B
Northern Ireland:	INI a, d

Investigation summary

Children insert a small funnel into the neck of a plastic bottle and seal around it with Blu-tack. They then pour water slowly into the funnel. They observe what happens.

Tips

You need to use very small funnels with straight, narrow spouts, otherwise the investigation might not work. Make sure children place their bottle on a firm, level surface, and keep it as still as possible.

Expected results

The water will not run into the bottle, or at least will have trouble doing so.

Explanation

Although the bottle looks empty, it is crammed full of air atoms which occupy all the space inside. There is very little room for the air to escape since the funnel has a small spout, so when the water is poured into the funnel, there is little or no space for it in the bottle, and it creates a seal which stops any more air escaping. This is why the water gets 'stuck' in the funnel. This result is aided by one of the properties of water: surface tension. The water molecules (several atoms bonded together) are held together by powerful forces. In some funnels, the water will 'sag' down into the bottle, almost as if it were in a sack.

Further ideas

Take two plastic bottles, and half-fill one of them with water. Join them together with the empty bottle at the top so they resemble an hourglass (cut the top of one bottle off just above the neck, insert the top of the other inside the hole, and then seal the join with silicone sealant or Blu-tack). Carefully turn the 'hourglass' over. The water will remain in the upper bottle, or at least it will run down very slowly. Big bubbles of air will grudgingly move upwards and the water will sporadically trickle down. Spinning the bottles will set the water in motion and create a beautiful whirlpool.

119

Dropping paper

 Hold up the two identical pieces of paper to the same height.

You will need:

two equal-sized pieces of paper

 Drop them both at the same time.

Do they hit the floor at about the same time?

How could you make them fall at different speeds?

 Try different ways to change the speed at which the paper falls. You may not cut or tear the paper or add anything else to it!

Did your investigation work? What did you do? What happened?

Dropping paper

Learning objective: to understand that air offers resistance

Curriculum links

England/Wales: KS2 Sc4 2c

Scotland: KUE C

Northern Ireland: KS2 KPF c

Investigation summary

Children try to change the speed at which two identical pieces of paper fall. They must make sure that their test is fair.

Tips

If the children can't think of a way to do this, prompt them by asking 'Could you make one piece smaller without making it lighter?'

Expected results

A folded or crumpled piece of paper will hit the floor before a flat sheet.

Explanation

Air provides resistance. The larger the area trying to push air atoms aside, the more air resistance there will be, and therefore the slower the object will move through the air. The following model may help the children to understand. Say to them: 'Imagine that you are all small atoms of air spread at random all over the room. I am the scrunched-up piece of paper.' (Put your arms against your sides.) 'I am small and don't occupy much space. Now I'm falling through the air.' (Walk around the classroom.) 'I don't bump into many of you because I don't take up much space.' (Spread your arms out wide.) 'Now I'm the flat sheet of paper. I'm falling through the air.' (Walk around the classroom.) 'I bump into more of you than before because I take up more space. The more air atoms I bump into, the more it slows me down.'

Everyday examples

A parachute is an example of how we use air resistance to help us. You can make a model of a parachute using a handkerchief, a key and some string.

There are many examples of air resistance in the sporting world. Downhill skiers crouch down to reduce air resistance. Cyclists reduce air resistance by wearing smoothly shaped helmets, having their handlebars set very low, and riding with their heads low down.

The air cannon

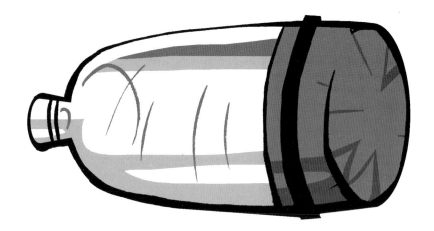

You will need:

an air cannon made from a plastic bottle and a balloon

  1 Aim the air cannon at a friend's hair and tap the balloon base.

What happened?

  2 What else can you do with the air cannon? For example, can you move bits of paper? Try some different things.

How do you think the air cannon works?

The air cannon

Learning objective: to feel air in motion; to see the effect of a pressure

Curriculum links

England/Wales:	KS2 Sc4 2c
Scotland:	KUE C
Northern Ireland:	KS2 KPF c

Everyday examples

When a large truck enters a tunnel at speed, light objects such as litter inside the tunnel will start to move long before the truck reaches them. This is because as the truck enters the tunnel, a lot of air atoms are suddenly pushed very fast into a small space, creating a powerful pressure wave.

Sometimes when we are hot we use a magazine to fan ourselves. Waving the magazine back and forth pushes air atoms towards us, and we can feel a breeze on our faces.

Investigation summary

You will need to make the air cannons yourself, as it would not be safe for the children to make them themselves. For each one, take a large, plastic bottle and cut the bottom off. Cut out a circle from a balloon. Stretch the balloon section tightly over the bottom of the bottle, and secure with a strong rubber band.

Children experiment with the air cannons. They try aiming the air cannon at a friend's hair and tapping the stretched balloon, and then come up with their own ideas of things they could do with the cannon. This gives them an opportunity to come up with a lot of fun ideas, for example 'How far does the puff of air reach?' or 'Can I make the air bounce off a wall?' You can demonstrate for the class that the air cannon can blow out a candle.

Expected results

The wave of air produced by the air cannon can move things, make hair flutter, and blow out a candle.

Explanation

When you tap the balloon base, the atoms of air in the bottle are given a push (a force). This starts a chain reaction in which the air atoms continue to push each other in the same direction, like when you knock down the first domino in a row and they push each other over one by one. Lots of atoms gather at the mouth of the bottle and these push the few atoms that are gathered in the neck. This gives these atoms an extra-powerful push (because lots of atoms are pushing a few atoms). A strong pressure wave is created which moves through the room until it meets something that slows it down.

Ask children to imagine a row of balls (atoms) lying along the floor. If you push the first one into the second, the second will move and push the third, and so on. With each collision some of the force is lost, and so after a while the balls stop moving.

Balancing balloons

 Tie the string in the middle of the dowelling.

 Peg a clothes peg to each end of the dowelling.

 Hang the two balloons from one end of the dowelling using the clothes peg.
Do not blow up the balloons!

 One person holds the dowelling up by the string. Someone else moves the peg without the balloons until the dowelling hangs straight.

Carefully remove the balloons and blow them up as much as you can.

What do you think will happen if you hang the inflated balloons where they were before?

 Hang the balloons back in the same position as they were before.

Were you right?

 Draw and describe what happened.

Is that what you expected?

Balancing balloons

Learning objective: to understand that air has mass

Curriculum links

England/Wales: Sc1 2b, 2i

Scotland: SIS B

Northern Ireland: INI d

Further ideas

When the balloons are inflated and have weighed down the balloon scales, you can then do the investigation backwards, i.e. by letting the air out. First make a small cross out of tape on each of the balloons and balance the scales. Carefully prick a hole with a needle through the tape and let the air seep out. After a while, you will see that the balloon side has become lighter.

When the holes are made in the balloons they in effect turn into small jet motors and will spin around a bit. If you'd like to further explore this effect, you can take the opportunity to make a balloon rocket! Tie a relatively fine length of string from one side of the classroom to the other, or up a flight of stairs. Thread a straight drinking straw onto the string. Wrap some sticky tape around two sections of the straw, twisting the tape half-way through so that the sticky side is facing outwards. Inflate a balloon and stick it to the pieces of tape. Do not tie the end! Release the balloon and it will shoot along the string.

Investigation summary

Children make a balloon scale by tying a piece of string around the middle of a piece of dowelling, putting a clothes peg on each end, and attaching two deflated balloons to one end using one of the pegs. They adjust the position of the non-balloon peg until the scale is balanced. They then remove the balloons, blow them up, and think about what will happen when they are put back in the same position. They try it, and see what happens.

Tips

This investigation works best with really long pieces of dowelling and large balloons inflated as much as possible. Remind children not to stand too close to the inflated balloons as they are very sensitive to static electricity!

Expected results

The scales will no longer be balanced when the inflated balloons are hung up. The balloons are heavier when they are inflated than when they were deflated.

Explanation

Although we often think of air as being weightless, it does in fact have mass. Everything that consists of matter has mass. Of course in this investigation we don't find out the exact mass of air, but it is actually about 1.3 grams per litre. A quick mental calculation will show that the air in a small room has about as much mass as a 6-year-old child! Feel free to work out the total mass of the air in your classroom.

Home investigation

The bag and the books

 Lay the plastic bag on the table.

 Place a book on top of it.
Make sure you can reach the bag's opening.

 Blow up the bag as if it were a balloon.

How many *books* you can lift?

 Draw a picture and explain what happens in the bag.

You will need:

a plastic food bag
with no holes

several books

a table

Home investigation teacher notes

The bag and the books

Investigation summary

Children place a book on top of an empty plastic food bag with no holes. They then inflate the bag and see what happens. They investigate how many books they can lift.

Expected results

The books will be lifted by the inflated bag.

Explanation

Air atoms take up space. They fill the bag, making it larger, and the books are pushed upwards. When you blow into the bag, the pressure underneath the books increases and exceeds the force pressing them down onto the table (gravity).

Everyday examples

Lifting things with air has a lot of technical applications. Many moving parts in machines are actually moved by air. You've no doubt heard the whooshing sound when a bus closes its door – that's the air in the moving parts doing its job.

Further investigations

A stick under a newspaper

You will need: a double-page sheet from a broadsheet newspaper; a piece of thin dowelling about 30 cm long

Investigation

This investigation is best done as a demonstration. Lay a newspaper out on a table so the edges are flush with the edge of the tabletop. Insert the stick under the middle of the newspaper so that half of the stick is hanging out over the edge of the table. Smooth out the newspaper carefully so that it is lying completely flat. Hit the end of the stick fast and hard with the side of your hand.

Expected results

Most children will expect the stick to fly off the table, taking the newspaper with it, but in fact the stick will break, while the newspaper hardly moves.

Explanation

Air pressure holds the newspaper in place. The newspaper has a large surface area, and the larger the surface area, the more air atoms will be pushing down on it. This is enough to hold it in place. Because the newspaper stops the stick from lifting quickly enough, the stick snaps in two. When you smoothed down the newspaper this made sure that there was hardly any air underneath it. If there had been a lot of air underneath it, the air would have helped to lift the paper up when you hit the stick, and the stick would have lifted up rather than breaking.

A short history of...

The four elements

Remember that the ancient Greeks believed that all matter was made up of four elements: earth, air, fire and water? They also believed that each of these elements behaved in particular ways because of where they come from. For example, earth comes from the ground, so the philosophers believed that a stone dropped when it was thrown because it wanted to return to the earth. Similarly, they thought that the reason air rises was because its 'home' was the sky, and so it would always try to return there.

The first barometer

The Italian physicist Evangelista Torricelli (1608–1647) showed that when a glass tube containing mercury was turned upside down, an airless space (a vacuum) was formed above the mercury. He also noted that the column of mercury varied in length from day to day. He proposed the theory that it was air that held the mercury in the tube. He failed to realise that this was the effect of changing air pressure, or that what he had in fact built was a barometer.

Blaise Pascal

Inspired by the work of Torricelli, the Frenchman Blaise Pascal (1623–1662) later performed similar experiments. Pascal used liquids other than mercury, such as water and red wine, and also performed the experiments at different altitudes. The results were so clear-cut that he became convinced that it was air pressure that was acting upon the fluids.

Two copper domes

When the German physicist and inventor Otto von Guericke (1602–1686) wanted to demonstrate the power of air pressure, he used more drastic methods. He placed two large copper hemispheres together and then pumped the air out of them (creating a vacuum). The air pressure held them together with such force that not even sixteen horses, eight in each direction, could pull them apart. These copper hemispheres are commonly known as Magdeburg hemispheres. You can replicate this experiment, but fortunately you won't need any horses – just two plungers!

Investigation	Curriculum links

Classroom investigations

Musical instruments
to understand how to produce notes from a variety of musical instruments

Sc4 3c: that there are many kinds of sound and sources of sound
KS2 Sc4 3e: that sounds are made when objects vibrate but that vibrations are not always directly visible
KUF B: link light and sound to seeing and hearing
KUF C: link sound to sources of vibration
KPS c: investigate how sounds are produced when objects vibrate

A bottle drum
to understand that the vibrations produced when you sing can make other things vibrate

Sc4 3c: that there are many kinds of sound and sources of sound
KS2 Sc4 3e: that sounds are made when objects vibrate but that vibrations are not always directly visible
KUF B: link light and sound to seeing and hearing
KUF C: link sound to sources of vibration
KPS a: listen to and investigate sources of sounds in their immediate environment
KPS c: investigate how sounds are produced when objects vibrate

A rockin' ruler
to understand how to alter the pitch and volume of a sound produced by a vibrating object

Sc4 3c: that there are many kinds of sound and sources of sound
KS2 Sc4 3e: that sounds are made when objects vibrate but that vibrations are not always directly visible
KUF B: link light and sound to seeing and hearing
KUF C: link sound to sources of vibration
KPS b: explore ways of making sounds using familiar objects

A tuning fork
to see and feel how a note is generated when something vibrates

Sc4 3c: that there are many kinds of sound and sources of sound
KS2 Sc4 3e: that sounds are made when objects vibrate but that vibrations are not always directly visible
KUF C: link sound to sources of vibration
KPS c: investigate how sounds are produced when objects vibrate

A spoon in your ear
to show that some things conduct sound better than others

Sc4 3c: that there are many kinds of sound and sources of sound
KUF C: link sound to sources of vibration
KPS b: explore ways of making sounds using familiar objects
KPS c: investigate how sounds are produced when objects vibrate

Home investigations

String instrument

Further investigations

Making a bullroarer

Sound like Donald Duck

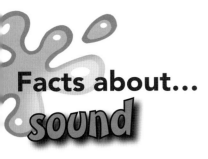

Facts about...

sound

Sounds and vibrations

Sound occurs when something moves or vibrates. It might be your vocal cords, a drum skin or a guitar string. When something vibrates, the air atoms around it vibrate. This sets up a chain of movement of air atoms, until the air reaches your ears, where it makes your eardrum vibrate, allowing you to hear the sound.

Volume and pitch

It is important to remember that pitch and volume are different. The pitch is how high or low a sound is, and this is affected by how fast the object that causes the sound vibrates. The volume is how loud or quiet the sound is. We measure pitch in Hertz (Hz), which measures frequency. The slowest vibrations that can be detected by the human ear are 20 Hz and the fastest 20 000 Hz. Many animals can detect frequencies well beyond human capabilities. Volume is measured in decibels (dB). Normal conversation is about 60 dB. Very loud sounds can damage our hearing. Listening to something at 100 dB for just ten minutes can produce permanent damage. Music at clubs or concerts is often louder than this!

Travelling through different materials

Our ears can also hear vibrations through liquids and solids, for example when you swim underwater in a swimming pool or when you lie on your side in bed with your ear pressed to the mattress, and hear it creaking as you move. Surprisingly, sound travels better through liquids than through air, and better through solids than through liquids. This is because the particles in solids are closer together than those in liquids, and those in liquids are closer together than those in air. When the particles are closer together, it is easier for a vibration to be passed between them.

It may not seem to make sense that solids are the best sound conductors, since we shut doors to keep sound out. Think about how voices sound muffled from the next room if you press your ear against the wall! But this is because the sound is travelling through two different materials – air and a solid. When sound has to change media in this way, the vibrations aren't carried as well. Curtains work very well to insulate a room against sound, as fabric contains tiny air pockets, so sounds have to pass through different layers of fabric and air, which forces them to change medium many times.

A noisy picture

Notes on the picture

The sounds Jamie can hear

Jamie is listening to all the sounds he can hear from his bedroom. Inside the house, he can hear his step-dad flushing the toilet, his mum dropping a saucepan on the floor, his sister drying her hair, the washing machine spinning, and the canary, dog, cat and goldfish all making noises. In the street he can hear Meena ringing on the doorbell and a woman in high heels walking on the pavement.

Sound conductors

Some materials conduct sound better than others. A pillow that is thick and fluffy is a poor conductor and acts as a muffler instead. Jamie can hear all the sounds well because he is lying on his back, rather than on his side with one ear pressed into the pillow. The water in the fish tank is a good sound conductor, so Jamie can hear the very quiet sound his goldfish makes. Metal is another good sound conductor, so you can hear the sound of water running a long way down the metal pipes when the toilet is flushed.

Musical instruments

You will need:

several different
musical
instruments

 Try to get the instruments to make some sound.

 Listen carefully to the different sounds.

 Feel each instrument when it is being played.

Did you feel anything?

What do you think makes each instrument produce sounds?

Do you think all instruments work in the same way?

How do you play different notes?

 Draw and describe all the things you found out.

Musical instruments

Learning objective: to understand how to produce notes from a variety of musical instruments

Curriculum links

England/Wales:	Sc4 3c;
	KS2 Sc4 3e
Scotland:	KUF B, C
Northern Ireland:	KPS c

Investigation summary

Give the children a selection of musical instruments to look at. Children should see if they can make sounds with them. They should then feel an instrument while it is being played. They should think about how each instrument produces sound, and how you play different notes.

Tips

This activity works just as well with inexpensive toy instruments. Alternatively, you could perform the activity as a demonstration.

Try to have at least one instrument from each of the following categories: string, woodwind and free-reed (e.g. a harmonica or accordion).

Expected results

Children should be able to feel some vibration when each instrument is played. Children are likely to discover how to play different notes on some of the instruments.

Explanation

The strings on a guitar or the air in a woodwind instrument vibrate and set the air atoms in motion. This makes sound. The air vibrates back and forth at the same rate as the string, which moves approximately 0.0001 mm. A chain reaction occurs with one atom pushing the next.

Musical notes are formed when the vibrations are regular. When air atoms vibrate irregularly we experience the sound as noise, rather than music. The higher the rate of vibration, the higher the pitch of the note. This is achieved in string instruments by either shortening or tightening the string. The same effect is achieved in woodwind instruments by shortening the column of air. If you play with more force, the note produced will be louder.

Further ideas

If you like, you can also ask the children make their own instruments. Here are some ideas:

a) a piece of wire stretched between two pins

b) a selection of bottles filled with different amounts of water

c) a drinking straw with the end cut off (making the straw shorter alters the pitch).

A bottle drum

 1 Point the air cannon at a friend's hair and tap the balloon base.

You will need:

an air cannon made from a plastic bottle and a balloon

salt

What happens? Can you explain why this happens?

 2 Hold the air cannon between your thumb and two fingers.

3 Hold the air cannon near your mouth and try singing different notes. Sing loud, long notes!

What happens? Try to explain it.

 4 Turn the air cannon upside down and sprinkle a few grains of salt onto the balloon base.

 5 Hold the air cannon quite close to your mouth and sing a few notes. Don't put your mouth too close to the salt.

What happens to the salt? Can you explain why this happens?

A bottle drum

Learning objective: to understand that the vibrations produced when you sing can make other things vibrate

Curriculum links

England/Wales:	Sc4 3c;
	KS2 Sc4 3e
Scotland:	KUF B, C
Northern Ireland:	KPS a, c

Make sure children do not have their faces too close to the air cannon when the salt is on the balloon base.

Investigation summary

You will need to make some air cannons for this lesson by cutting the bottoms off some large, plastic bottles, stretching balloon sections over the ends, and securing them with thick rubber bands. Make sure the balloons are stretched tightly with no wrinkles.

Children try tapping the balloon base while aiming the air cannon at a friend's hair. Next, they try singing with their mouths close to the balloon base. They then try putting a few grains of salt on the base and singing again.

Expected results

When the children point the air cannon at a friend's hair and strike the balloon base, the hair will move. When children sing close to the air cannon, it will emit a ghostly echo, as if it is singing along with them! They will be able to feel the bottle vibrating. When children sing close to the air cannon with salt on the base, the salt will jump around.

Explanation

When the balloon base is struck, air atoms are pushed into other air atoms, and when they pass through the narrow neck of the bottle, a powerful pressure wave is created, allowing the air to move someone's hair. You can use this to help children connect the ideas of pressure waves and sound waves.

When you sing, you push air. Your vocal chords vibrate inside your throat and they are stretched or relaxed to vary the pitch of the notes you sing. This can be compared to letting the air out of a balloon while you stretch and relax the opening. Singing close to the balloon base sets not only the air in motion, but also the balloon itself. This can be seen very clearly when the salt starts jumping around. This phenomenon is called resonance and many instruments have a resonance chamber that amplifies the sound by pushing more air atoms. The eardrums in our ears work in the same way, vibrating in response to different sounds.

A rockin' ruler

You will need:

a ruler

things to muffle
sound with

 Place the ruler on a table so half of it is
hanging over the side.

 Hold the ruler down hard with your
thumb at the edge of the table.

 Pluck the end
of the ruler
to make it vibrate.

 Try to make different notes.

How did you do this?

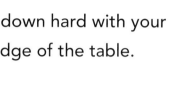 Try to make the notes louder or softer.

How did you do this?

 Place different things between the ruler and the table.

How does this change the sound?

 Draw and describe what you did and what happened.
Try to explain your results.

A rockin' ruler

Learning objective: to understand how to alter the pitch and volume sound produced by a vibrating object

Curriculum links

England/Wales:	Sc4 3c;
	KS2 Sc4 3e
Scotland:	KUF B, C
Northern Ireland:	KPS b

Investigation summary

Children place a ruler half on and half off a table, and hold it down firmly at the edge of the table. They then gently pluck the end. They try to make different notes, and to make the notes louder or softer. Finally, they try placing different materials, such as cloth or paper, between the ruler and the table, to change the sound.

Tips

The ruler should not be too floppy. To avoid broken rulers, use wooden rulers or thin bits of wood. Good mufflers are newspaper, wool and cotton.

Expected results

Children will be able to feel the ruler vibrating when the end of the ruler is plucked, and they will hear a twanging sound. They can change the pitch of the sound by moving more or less of the ruler over the edge of the table. The shorter the length of ruler hanging over the side, the higher the pitch will be. Children can change the volume of the sound by bending the ruler more or less. If you bend the ruler more you will get a louder note. Fabric or paper between the table and the ruler muffle the sound.

Explanation

When the ruler is plucked, it begins to vibrate, which pushes the air atoms around it. The vibrations of the ruler are regular which is why the sound produced is perceived as a note. A short length of ruler produces a note of a higher pitch because it vibrates faster. This is referred to as a higher frequency and is measured in vibrations per second. The cloth and paper muffle the sound because they are soft materials that do not vibrate along with the ruler. If you were to place the ruler against a piano or guitar the sound would be amplified. The body of a guitar provides excellent resonance.

A tuning fork

1 Hold the tuning fork as shown in the picture.

You will need:

a tuning fork

a beaker of water

2 Carefully tap one of the prongs against something.

3 Try holding the tuning fork against different things while it is vibrating to see if you can make the sound louder.

What things make the sound louder?

4 Make the fork vibrate and press it against your head close to your ear.

What happens to the sound? Why do you think this is?

5 Make the fork vibrate and dip it into the beaker of water.

What happens?

A tuning fork

Learning objective: to see and feel how a note is generated when something vibrates

Curriculum links

England/Wales:	Sc4 3c;
	KS2 Sc4 3e
Scotland:	KUF C
Northern Ireland:	KPS c

Investigation summary

Children try making a tuning fork vibrate by tapping it on something. They then try to make the sound louder by holding it against other things. Next, they hold the vibrating fork against their heads, near the ear. Lastly, they dip the vibrating fork into a beaker of water.

Tips

You can buy a tuning fork from any music shop.

Expected results

Some of the things that will amplify the note are: a desk top, a window pane, a guitar, a piano or an empty box. When the tuning fork is pressed against the ear or the bone behind the ear, the note will sound louder. When the tuning fork is dipped into water, ripples can be seen in the water.

Explanation

The tuning fork's vibrations are regular and therefore produce a note. The sound is amplified when the fork is held against a solid object such as a desk top because the entire surface of the desk top will resonate with the fork, which means that it is also creating waves in the air. The more pressure waves are travelling through the air, the louder the sound will be. Air is a poor conductor of sound. This is why the sound of the tuning fork gets louder when it is pressed against your head. You can create a longer 'bone conductor' by sticking your finger in your ear and then pressing the vibrating tuning fork against your elbow. The fact that bone conducts sound better than air explains why most hearing aids are actually placed behind the ear. Sound waves travel more quickly through water than through air, and because we can see water, we can also see the effects of the pressure waves passing through it. Another way of seeing the vibrations is to hang a ping-pong ball from a string and then touch it with the vibrating tuning fork.

A spoon in your ear

 Tie the thread around the spoon, leaving an equal length of thread on either side.

 Wind the ends of the thread around your index fingers.

 Press your fingers hard against your ears. The spoon will dangle down in front of you.

 Walk around the classroom and let the spoon hit different things.

You will need:

a piece of thread 120 cm long

a metal spoon

What does it sound like?

 Take the thread away from your ears.

 Knock the spoon against different things.

What does it sound like now?

 Try to explain why it sounds different.

A spoon in your ear

Learning objective: to show that some things conduct sound better than others

Curriculum links

England/Wales: Sc4 3c

Scotland: KUF C

Northern Ireland: KPS b, c

Everyday examples

The Native Americans used to put their ear to the ground to hear hoof beats. You have probably seen Western films where train robbers listen to the railway tracks to hear when the train is coming. There are also many examples of how prison inmates communicated with each other by tapping the walls. Let the children try by tapping radiators and listening in distant rooms, or tapping on the water pipes, which works extremely well.

Water is also a good sound conductor. This allows whales to communicate with each other over great distances. You could play a tape of whale sounds to the class to illustrate this example.

Further ideas

You could extend the thread and spoon experiment by investigating the effects of using different types of thread, for example coarse string or picture wire. The results will be quite different and this leads to the conclusion that certain materials are better sound conductors than others.

Investigation summary

Children each use a metal spoon tied in the centre of a long piece of cotton thread (about 120 cm). They wrap the ends of the thread around their index fingers, and press their index fingers against their ears. They then walk around the classroom and allow their spoons to knock into things, and listen to the sounds. Then, they investigate how the sound differs when they don't have their fingers against their ears.

Expected results

If you get it just right the spoon will sound just like a church bell. The sound will seem quieter to the children when they take their fingers away from their ears and make the sounds again.

Explanation

Metal is an excellent conductor, so a metal spoon will make a good sound when knocked against other solid objects. The thread conducts the sound better than air (because sound travels better through a solid than through a gas). The atoms that make up the thread push each other and the chain reaction reaches all the way up to your ear.

Home investigation

String instrument

 Try to make a string instrument out of the box and rubber bands.

How do you produce different notes?

You will need:

an empty box or small carton

rubber bands of different sizes and strengths

 Try to make the notes louder or softer.

How did you do it?

 Bring your instrument to school and explain to the class what you did.

Home investigation teacher notes

String instrument

Investigation summary

Children make a string instrument using an empty box or carton and rubber bands of different sizes and strengths. They investigate how to make different notes, and how to make the notes louder and softer.

Expected results

Different types of box produce different types of sound. The tighter the rubber band is stretched, the higher the pitch. A thicker rubber band will have a lower pitch. Children can make the notes louder or softer by plucking the bands harder or more gently. Some children may discover that if they put something in the box, such as cotton wool, the sound will be 'dampened'.

Explanation

The 'string instruments' will make notes because the rubber bands vibrate when plucked, and set the air atoms around them in motion. The air vibrates back and forth at the same rate as the rubber band. If you can change the speed at which the band vibrates, you can change the note. The faster the band vibrates, the higher the pitch of the note will be. A tighter band will vibrate more quickly, so tighter bands produce high notes, just like when you shorten the string on a guitar by moving your finger along the neck closer to the body of the guitar.

Further investigations

Making a bullroarer

You will need: a cork cut in half; a thin piece of dowelling; a thick rubber band; some thick paper; scissors; sticky tape; 1m of string

Investigation

The children should be able to do most of the construction themselves, but it is best if you cut the corks in half yourself, using a knife, and then make a hole through each half using a skewer. Children can then push one half of the cork onto each end of their piece of dowelling. They then take a rubber band and stretch it all the way from the end of one cork to the end of the other, so it runs parallel to the dowelling. Children then cut out a wing shape from thick paper (they could decorate these with paint if there is time). They attach their wing along the length of their dowelling using sticky tape. Finally, they tie a long piece of string around one end of the dowelling, just above the cork. Now they can try out their bullroarers – find a space away from everyone else and swing it around their heads!

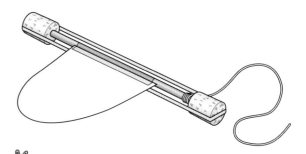

Expected results

As the name suggests, the bullroarer will make a 'roaring' or whirring sound. Different types of rubber band will produce different sounds.

Further ideas

A bullroarer is an instrument used by the Aborigines in Australia as a message-sending device. A real bullroarer is made out of a piece of wood or bone about two feet long, attached to a piece of hide or skin.

Sound like Donald Duck

You will need: a helium balloon

Investigation

Demonstrate to the children what happens when you breathe in some helium, and then speak. Although the children will probably be very keen to try this for themselves, it is not recommended as there is a slight risk involved. Your body has no use for helium, so while your lungs are filled with helium, you are not taking in any oxygen. As long as you keep breathing, though, it should be fine. Of course, you may not be willing to try this investigation yourself, in which case a discussion of the effects of helium on the voice would work fine.

WARNING! Never inhale helium from a canister. Helium from a canister is under high pressure, and will expand rapidly when it is released.

Expected results

Your voice will be high and squeaky, like Donald Duck or a cartoon chipmunk!

Explanation

Helium is thinner than air (it has a lower density). When vocal chords vibrate in a gas that is thinner than air, they vibrate much faster. This results in a higher pitch (more vibrations per second, higher frequency).

A short history of...
sound

The Greeks tune up

The nature of sound was something that the Greek philosophers thought long and hard about. Pythagoras (c. 560–500 BC) performed an experiment that resembled modern scientific experiments when he investigated the sound produced by strings of varying length and thickness. He also simultaneously plucked two strings of the same size and varied their lengths to see when they sounded dissonant (out of tune). He discovered that when the relation between the strings was 1:2 or 1:4 or 3:4, in other words ratios of whole numbers, a pleasing harmony was produced. His conclusions led to the development of the musical scale system that we use today.

The first telephone

The first successful attempt to convert sound waves into electrical vibrations was made by a German schoolteacher by the name of Phillip Reis (1834–1874). He attached a platinum plate and metal spring to a membrane made out of sausage skin. The platinum was connected to a power source and when someone spoke or sang into the sausage skin the sound waves were converted into electrical vibrations. It was by no means a working telephone but at least it was now possible to send sounds in one direction. Alexander Graham Bell (1847–1922) and Elisha Gray (1835–1901) developed Reis's invention to create the telephone.

The silent bell

It had long been theorised that sound was some kind of wave and that its vibrations were propagated by the movement of air. In 1650, Otto von Guericke (1602–1686) proved that these ideas were on the right track. He placed a bell in a container and pumped out all the air to create a vacuum. There was no longer any air to transport the sound waves and as a result the bell could not be heard.

The first gramophone

Thomas Edison (1847–1931) was the first person to successfully store sound. He christened the recording machine that he built in 1877 the 'phonograph'. One end of a needle was attached to the end of a paper funnel, and the other rested against a soft wax cylinder that was coated with a thin layer of metal. When someone sang into the funnel it vibrated in time with the song. These vibrations were transferred to the needle, which in turn transferred them to the revolving cylinder in the form of a long wobbly groove. When the wax had set, the needle could be placed in the groove and the cylinder revolved. The needle vibrated in time with the groove and caused the funnel to vibrate. The funnel set the surrounding air molecules in motion and soon the sound waves could be heard. The vibrations were identical to what was sung into the funnel in the first place so this is what was heard when it was played back.

Investigation	**Curriculum links**

Classroom investigations

Why do we see?
to understand that we see light sources because they emit light and other things because they reflect light

Sc4 3a: to identify different light sources, including the Sun
Sc4 3b: that darkness is the absence of light
KUF B: link light and sound to seeing and hearing
KPL a: find out that light comes from a variety of sources

A dark room and a torch
to understand that we see light sources because they emit light and other things because they reflect light

Sc4 3a: to identify different light sources, including the Sun
Sc4 3b: that darkness is the absence of light
KUF B: link light and sound to seeing and hearing
KUF C: give examples of light being reflected from surfaces
KPL a: find out that light comes from a variety of sources

A shining torch
to understand that light travels in a straight line

Sc4 3a: to identify different light sources, including the Sun
KS2 Sc4 3a: that light travels from a source
KUF C: give examples of light being reflected from surfaces
KPL a: find out that light comes from a variety of sources

A torch and a mirror
to see how light bounces off a flat mirror

Sc4 3a: to identify different light sources, including the Sun
KS2 Sc4: 3c: that light is reflected from surfaces
KUF C: give examples of light being reflected from surfaces
KPL c: explore how light passes through some materials and not others
KS2 KPL c: investigate the reflection of light from mirrors and other shiny surfaces

Lots of beams
to see how light bounces off a flat mirror

Sc4 3a: to identify different light sources, including the Sun
KS2 Sc4 3c: that light is reflected from surfaces
KUF C: give examples of light being reflected from surfaces
KPL c: explore how light passes through some materials and not others
KS2 KPL c: investigate the reflection of light from mirrors and other shiny surfaces

Home investigations

Remote control

Further investigations

Shadow puppets

Two mirrors

Facts about...

The Sun and the moon

The Sun is the primary light source on Earth. It is a giant ball of fire which is 6000°C on its surface. It emits light, which travels at the incredible speed of 300 000 kilometres per second. This means that light from the Sun takes 8 minutes to reach the earth. It often looks as though the moon is shining, but it doesn't actually give out light. The light we see is reflected from the Sun.

Shadows

Light travels in straight lines. One piece of evidence for this is the way in which shadows are formed. When light meets an opaque object, the light can pass all around the object, but not through it. When the light that passes around the sides of the object meets a surface such as the ground or a wall, we can see the light, and the 'hole' in it that was created by the object. The shape of this 'hole' will be very similar to the shape of the object itself. Sundials make use of shadows to show us the time. As the Earth turns, the shadow cast by the stick or wedge in the centre of the sundial will move around in a circle, which tells us what time of day it is.

Rainbows

Scientists call the light that comes from the Sun 'white light'. Sunlight isn't actually white at all, but is made up of seven different colours: red, orange, yellow, green, blue, indigo and violet. We can't usually see these colours separately. One of the occasions we can see these colours is when a rainbow appears in the sky. Rainbows occur when it is raining and sunny at the same time. When sunlight meets a raindrop, the light is bent around the curved drop, and it splits into its seven colours. This process is called diffraction. A rainbow is actually a circle; we only see half of it. A circle has no end, which is why you can never find a pot of gold at the end of a rainbow!

Invisible light

There are some types of light that humans can't see, for example ultra-violet light and infra-red light. Insects such as bees and butterflies can see ultra-violet light.

THE LIGHT FANTASTIC

Meena and Jamie are watching television.

Do you want to see a trick?

Maybe later.

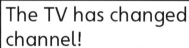
The TV has changed channel!

How did you do that? Put it back.

I know how you're doing that! I can do it too.

Why isn't it working?

Notes on the story

The remote control

Remote controls emit light that humans can't see (infra-red). This light bounces (reflects) in exactly the same way as the light we can see.

The mirror

Light travels in a straight line. If it hits a reflective surface such as a mirror, it gets bounced off at an angle. Jamie uses the mirror to bounce the beam from the hallway to the television. This is how he is able to change the channel without being in the room.

The piece of paper

A piece of paper is fairly thin, so the remote control beam passes through it and Jamie is still able to change the channel. If you hold a piece of thin paper up to the window or a lamp, you can see that some light passes through it.

The book

Meena tries to prove that she can do the trick too, but she makes a mistake when she chooses a book to hide the remote control behind. A book is too thick to allow the beam of infra-red light to travel through, and so she is unable to change the channel.

Why do we see?

 Go out into the playground and look at the school buildings.

Can you explain why you can *see* the school?

 Draw the way you think light moves.

Can you explain why you can *see* the Sun? NEVER look directly at it!

What do you think would happen if the Sun went out?

152

Why do we see?

Learning objective: to understand that we see light sources because they emit light and other things because they reflect light

Curriculum links

England/Wales:	Sc4 3a, 3b
Scotland:	KUF B
Northern Ireland:	KPL a

Make sure children do not look directly at the Sun as there is a danger of permanent damage to their eyes.

Background knowledge

In order for the students to be able to understand optical phenomena it is vital that they are aware of the following:

1. Light is something that physically spreads out in the room even though this may not be visible.
2. The physical process of sight is initiated when light interacts with our retinas.

Investigation summary

Take the children out into the playground and ask them to look at the school buildings. Ask them to think about why they can see the buildings, and why they can see the Sun. They should think about what would happen if the Sun 'went out'!

Tips

Ask the children to draw themselves, the school buildings and the Sun on a sheet of paper. Children usually draw the Sun with rays showing the path of the sunlight. This is exactly the way physicists draw them!

You could miss out the questions about the Sun if you feel they are too leading.

Expected results

Here are a few examples of children's reasoning on the phenomenon of sight:

'The eye is active.'

'There has to be light to be able to see.'

'The eyes emit rays of light.'

'Light bounces back and forth between the eye and the object being seen.'

'Light travels from the seen object to the eye.'

Many children will answer that the earth would become dark and cold if the Sun were to go out.

Explanation

The Sun is a great ball of fire (it is 6000°C on its surface), and it emits light. Light is a form of energy. Light travels in straight lines in the form of rays. Some of the Sun's rays bounce off objects such as the school buildings and into our eyes. When this light hits our retinas, nerve impulses are sent to the brain. The picture is interpreted, and we 'see' the buildings.

If the Sun ceased to exist, the Earth would become cold and dark within a few hours. We would still be able to see things by artificial lights, but plants would stop photosynthesising, and after a few days all the rivers, lakes and seas would freeze.

A dark room and a torch

 Go into a completely dark room and shine the torch on a few different things.

You will need:

a completely dark room

a torch

Can you explain why you can *see* the things that the torch shines on?

 Draw and explain what you think happens.

A dark room and a torch

Learning objective: to understand that we see light sources because they emit light and other things because they reflect light

Curriculum links

England/Wales: Sc4 3a, 3b

Scotland: KUF B, C

Northern Ireland: KPL a

Investigation summary

Find a room that you can make very dark. Ask children to go in with a torch and shine it on some things in the room. Children must try to explain why they can see the things that the torch shines on, and then draw what they think happens.

Tips

A torch whose beam can be narrowed is best for this investigation. Making the room completely dark is not usually possible, but a little light doesn't matter. You can even use it in your reasoning process. The room might have to be a cupboard!

Expected results

Expect this type of drawing:

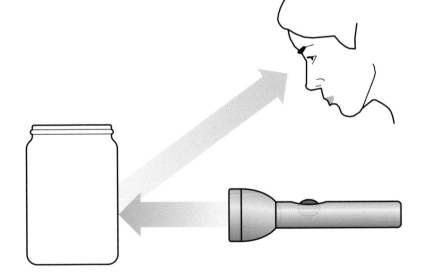

Everyday examples

Ask your class to look at home and see what sort of lights they have. How do lights constructed for different purposes differ? Make sure children know that they must not touch electrical devices unless supervised.

Further ideas

Once the children have drawn their pictures and explained how light behaves, make the classroom as dark as possible and light a candle. This is a good opportunity to consider the following:
What were the first light sources used by man?
How did electric lighting change people's lives?

Explanation

The filament in the torch is hot and emits light. The torch is a light source. The light it emits can bounce off objects and hit our retinas, allowing us to see the object. More light bounces off light-coloured objects than dark-coloured ones.

A shining torch

 Stand the cardboard up on the sheet of paper with the slot pointing down.

 Shine the torch at different angles through the slot.

 Draw some pictures to show the way the light looks on the other side of the cardboard.

 Describe what the light does.

What do you think would happen if you held one hand 10 cm from a wall and shone a torch on it? What do you think you would see on the wall?

 Draw what you think you would see.

 Try it and see if you were right!

What happened? Can you explain why this happens?

What do you think would happen if you moved your hand further away?

A shining torch

Learning objective: to understand that light travels in a straight line

Curriculum links

England/Wales:	Sc4 3a;
	KS2 Sc4 3a
Scotland:	KUF C
Northern Ireland:	KPL a

Investigation summary

You will need to prepare some of the materials for the children. Cut out one piece of cardboard, 15 cm by 15 cm, for each group of children. In the centre of one edge of each piece of cardboard, cut a slot roughly 5 mm by 6 cm. Children hold their piece of cardboard upright, with the slot pointing downwards, on top of a piece of white paper. One child shines a torch through the slot from different angles. Children observe what the light looks like on the other side of the cardboard, and draw pictures to show how it looks when the torch is shone from different angles.

Children then try holding their hand 10 cm in front of a wall and shining a torch at it. They investigate what happens if they move their hand further away from the wall.

Tips

It should be quite dark in the room when performing this investigation.

Expected results

The light will shine through the slot in a straight line from wherever it is pointed. The children's drawings should show this. Children usually draw light as straight rays resembling arrows, intuitively reflecting the way physicists themselves notate.

When you hold your hand in front of a wall, a shadow resembling your hand is formed. The closer to the wall you place your hand, the clearer the shadow becomes.

Explanation

Light travels in a straight line. If you place something opaque directly in front of the rays they will not pass through. A shadow in the shape of the obstacle is formed.

Further ideas

Let the children draw pictures of shadows of each other's heads. French minister Ètienne de Silhouette (1709–1767) used this technique to make paper cut-outs as a hobby, and we still use his name today when referring to this type of picture.

A torch and a mirror

 Stand the mirror up on the sheet of paper.

 Hold the cardboard in front of the mirror.

 Shine the torch through the slot in the cardboard. The light should hit the mirror.

You will need:

a small mirror

a sheet of white paper

a piece of cardboard with a slot cut into it

a torch

 Turn the mirror slightly.

What happens?

 Try turning the mirror at different angles.

 Draw the path of the light beam all the way from the torch to after it hits the mirror.

A torch and a mirror

Learning objective: to see how light bounces off a flat mirror

Curriculum links

England/Wales:	Sc4 3a;
	KS2 Sc4 3c
Scotland:	KUF C
Northern Ireland:	KPL c;
	KS2 KPL c

Investigation summary

You will need the squares of cardboard with the slots cut in the middle of one edge from the previous investigation (see page 157). Children hold a mirror upright at one end of a piece of white paper, with one of the pieces of cardboard at the other end, held parallel to the mirror. Another child shines a torch directly through the slot, so that it hits the mirror. The child holding the mirror turns it at different angles, and children observe what happens to the beam of light.

Tips

The point of the investigation is to make the light hit the mirror at different angles. Make sure the children understand the concept of angles before you start.

Expected results

Children will usually draw very simple diagrams like this:

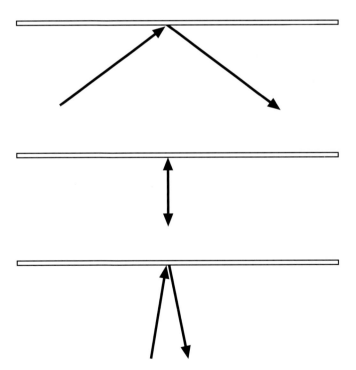

Explanation

Light always travels in a straight line. Light will therefore bounce off a mirror at the same angle as it hits it. Compare this to how a ball bounces against a wall. Feel free to demonstrate this.

Lots of beams

 Place the comb over the hole in the cardboard with the teeth pointing downwards.

 Use the sticky tape to hold the comb in place.

 Hold the cardboard upright on the sheet of paper.

 Shine the torch through the hole.

You will need:

a piece of cardboard with a hole

a comb

sticky tape

a sheet of white paper

a torch

a mirror

 Hold the mirror up behind the cardboard. The light should bounce off it.

 Turn the mirror at different angles.

What happens to the light beams?

 Draw pictures to show your results. Describe what you discovered.

Lots of beams

Learning objective: to see how light bounces off a flat mirror

Curriculum links

England/Wales:	Sc4 3a;
	KS2 Sc4 3c
Scotland:	KUF C
Northern Ireland:	KPL c;
	KS2 KPL c

Further ideas

Here is a fun investigation that requires a slightly bigger mirror. Place two identical glasses exactly the same distance from the mirror, one in front, and the other behind. Ask a child to look straight into the mirror. What they will see is the reflection of the glass that is in front of the mirror. If you have placed the glasses correctly, the reflected glass should seem to be the same distance away 'inside' the mirror as the other glass is behind the mirror. Give the child a small jug of water and ask them to fill the glass they can see in the mirror. The idea is that they should be able to tell where the glass behind the mirror is by using the reflection of the other glass as a guide. However, you should expect a bit of water to be spilt!

Investigation summary

You will need to prepare some of the materials for the children. Cut out one piece of cardboard, 15 cm by 15 cm, for each group of children. In the centre of one edge of each piece of cardboard, cut out a rectangular hole roughly 3 cm by 2 cm. Children tape a comb over the hole in their cardboard so that the teeth point downwards. One child holds it upright on a piece of white paper. Another child holds a mirror parallel to the cardboard. A third child shines a torch through the hole in the cardboard from different angles. Children then experiment with turning the mirror at different angles, and observing what happens to the light beams.

Tips

Dim the lights in the room. It is essential that the children produce a set of parallel beams, so make sure they try different angles and distances to get the best results.

Expected results

The light remains a set of parallel beams even after it has hit the mirror and regardless of how you angle the mirror.

Explanation

The light from the torch travels in a straight line. Some of it gets blocked by the teeth of the comb, so parallel lines of light travel between the teeth. These parallel lines continue in a straight line, and when they hit the mirror, they are reflected at the same angle as when they reached it. Therefore the lines will always remain parallel.

Home investigation

Remote control

 Investigate what happens when you hold something between the remote control and the appliance.

 Try different materials.

Through which materials does the remote control work?

You will need:

an appliance with a remote control (for example a television)

different materials: paper, foil, plastic, cloth, glass and wood

a mirror

 Try to get the beam from the remote control to bounce off a mirror towards the appliance.

How do you have to hold the mirror for this to work?

 Draw a picture to show this.

 Try to find out where the appliance receives the signal from the remote control.

What test did you do to find out?

 Describe your results. Draw pictures if you like.

Home investigation teacher notes

Remote control

Investigation summary

Children investigate holding different materials in between a remote control and an appliance (for example a television), to see which materials block the remote control beam, and which let it through. Children then try reflecting the beam off a mirror towards the appliance. Finally, they devise a way of finding the point at which the appliance receives the signal from the remote control.

Expected results

Aluminium foil, thick paper, wood and thick cloth will block the signal. Thin paper, thin cloth and glass will allow it to pass through. The mirror has to be held in a particular way to direct the signal to the appliance. Finding the sensor on the appliance may be a little harder, but children usually come up the idea of covering the appliance with one of the materials that blocked the signal. On certain appliances such as CD players the sensor may actually be marked, but you can still experiment with it. Give the children hints if necessary.

Explanation

The signal from the remote control is what is known as infra-red light. This is light with a frequency that humans can't see (although certain animals can see infra-red light). However, we can use this light to send information, in this case with the remote control where pushing different buttons sends different messages to the appliance. Light cannot pass through everything. It bounces (reflects) off certain materials such as the ones mentioned above. The light rays bounce off the mirror like a ball bouncing off a wall. This is the way light reflects off a flat mirror. The angle between the rays and the mirror is the same both before and after it bounces.

Further investigations

Shadow puppets

You will need: a white sheet; thick paper; scissors; fine dowelling, wooden skewers or cocktail sticks; overhead projector

Investigation

Hang a white sheet on the wall. Children cut out small paper figures and stick them onto fine sticks. They can even make figures with moving parts if they use several sticks! Direct the overhead projector towards the sheet, and switch it on. Children make their puppets move across the OHP plate and create a scene or short play.

Expected results

Highly entertaining shadow puppetry!

Explanation

Light travels in a straight line. When the light from the projector hits the puppets, they block the light and we see their silhouettes as black shapes on the sheet.

Two mirrors

You will need: two mirrors; an object

Investigation

Place two mirrors at an angle to each other, both reflecting inwards. Make the angle very wide. Place an object between the mirrors. What can the children see in the mirrors? Reduce the angle between the two mirrors. Children count how many images they can see. Keep gradually reducing the angle, and asking children to count the images.

Expected results

The smaller the angle between the mirrors, the more images can be seen.

Explanation

The light bounces off each mirror and onto the other. When the angle between them is wide, the light is then reflected away from the mirrors. When the angle is smaller, the light bounces between the mirrors more times, which produces more reflections. If the two mirrors were placed parallel to each other, the number of reflections would be infinite.

A short history of...
light

Greek thinking

Empedocles (fifth century BC) theorised that everything was composed of four elements: earth, air, fire and water. He believed that the human eye was made up of the four elements, and that sight was possible because of the fire shining out from the eyes. Because humans can't see very well in the dark, Empedocles knew that the phenomenon of sight must be more complicated than just light coming from the eyes. He postulated an interaction between light coming from the eyes and light coming from other sources, such as the Sun.

Euclid (c. 325–265 BC) discovered that light travels in straight lines. This discovery led to the system of navigation whereby one works out one's position based on the positions of the Sun and the stars.

Archimedes (287–212 BC) understood the way that a concave mirror can focus and concentrate light, and he used this knowledge to help fight his enemies. He lived on the island of Syracuse, which at that time was under threat from the Roman navy. Archimedes had a large mirror which he used to focus sunlight. In those days boats were made of wood and were powered by sails, so you can imagine what an effective weapon this was – it caused the enemy's boats to burst into flames before they could even reach land! But then again they could always come back on a cloudy day...

Middle-eastern thinking

Ibn al-Haytham (c. 965–1040) made the biggest breakthrough in ancient times into the study of light. He discounted earlier scientists' claims that our eyes emit light, and argued that we see things only because of light entering the eyes from outside sources. He believed that we see objects because rays of light travel in a straight line from the Sun, and are reflected off the objects and into our eyes. He also studied mirrors and lenses, and understood how refraction by a lens can focus and magnify things.

Newton sees the light

Englishman Isaac Newton (1642–1727), perhaps the most famous of all physicists on account of his theory of gravity, also studied optical phenomena. By making a small hole in a window shutter and letting the incoming light beam pass through a triangular piece of glass or prism, he managed to demonstrate that white light consists of, and could be separated into, the colours of the rainbow (the spectrum).

Lenses

These days, many people wear glasses to allow them to see better. Alexander the Great (356–323 BC) used a polished stone to see better with, and it is claimed that spectacles were being used in China over 2000 years ago. It was the Franciscan monk Roger Bacon (1214–1294) who first described how spectacles work. Unfortunately, short-sighted people who needed concave lenses to improve their sight had to wait a further 200 years!

It wasn't until the end of the 16th century that several lenses were combined to create powerfully magnified images. Binoculars and microscopes opened doors to worlds that had previously been beyond the reach of scientists. Galileo pointed his telescope at the heavens and observed things that led him to the revolutionary conclusion that the earth was not the centre of the Universe. Others concentrated their attention on the microscopic world, leading to important insights into disease and biological phenomena. Bacteria, cells and micro-organisms had previously been unknown to man because they were too small to be seen with the naked eye.

Investigation

Curriculum links

Classroom investigations

Rubbing balloons

to understand that you can charge things with static electricity, and that things with different charges are attracted to each other

Sc1 2a: ask questions and decide how they might find answers to them
Sc4 1a: about everyday appliances that use electricity
SIS B: use simple equipment and techniques to make observations and measurements
KUF A: give examples of everyday appliances that use electricity
INC a: make observations using their senses

Rubbing plastic bottles

to understand that statically charged objects can exert force on each other

Sc1 2a: ask questions and decide how they might find answers to them
Sc4 1a: about everyday appliances that use electricity
SIS B: use simple equipment and techniques to make observations and measurements
INC a: make observations using their senses

Can you light the bulb?

to understand that a light bulb will light up when it is part of a closed circuit

Sc4 1b: about simple series circuits involving batteries, wires, bulbs and other components
Sc4 1c: how a switch can be used to break a circuit
KUF C: construct simple battery-operated circuits, identifying the main components
KPE a: find out about some uses of electricity in the classroom
KS2 KPE b: construct simple circuits using components, such as switches, bulbs and batteries

Home investigations

Static bag

Further investigations

More static electricity

Facts about...
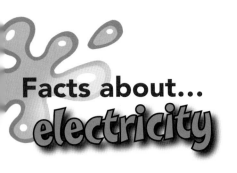

Static electricity

All atoms consist of three fundamental particles, two of which have electrical charges. Neutrons (found in the nucleus) have no charge. Protons (also found in the nucleus) have a positive charge. Electrons (found orbiting the nucleus) have a negative charge. When there are equal numbers of protons and electrons, the atom is electrically neutral. Static electricity is created when substances have an imbalance of protons and electrons. If a substance has more protons than electrons, it will be positively charged, and if it has more electrons than protons, it will be negatively charged.

If you put two positively charged or two negatively charged substances next to each other, they will be repelled from each other. If you put one positively charged substance next to a negatively charged one, they will be attracted to each other.

If you rub a piece of wool against a piece of polythene, electrons from the wool are rubbed off onto the polythene, leaving the wool positively charged and the polythene negatively charged, and so they are attracted to each other. Eventually, the extra electrons will leave the polythene and return to the wool.

Electrical circuits

An electric current is a flow of electrons along a conductor, such as a metal wire. An electrical circuit needs to be complete before an electric current will flow. Electric current does not get 'used up' because the electrons are not destroyed. Current is measure in amps. Electricity is a means of transferring energy.

Light bulbs

Light bulbs work by resisting the flow of the electrons. This causes the filament in the bulb to heat up and give out light.

Batteries

A battery is often used to give energy to an electrical circuit. A battery works by creating chemical reactions inside it, which release energy. Batteries have a positive and a negative pole. When a wire is connected between the two poles, one end of the wire becomes positively charged and the other end becomes negatively charged. This causes electrons to move through the wire towards the positive pole of the battery, where they are removed from the wire. While this is happening, the negative pole is giving out more electrons.

The substances used in an ordinary battery are carbon and zinc. In between these two substances is a substance that drives the flow of electrons, and a substance that stops the flow from staying inside the battery. The flow is forced out into an external circuit, for example through a wire or cable.

The Current family's house

Notes on the picture

Appliances and lights

There are many things in the picture that are connected with the subject of electricity. Challenge the children to find them all. How many appliances they can find? What are they? What about lights?

Batteries

Ask the children to consider which things in the picture run on batteries (for example the radio on the bedroom shelf, the torch on the kitchen table). How many other things can they think of that use batteries? (for example alarm clocks, toys, remote controls, telephones)

Static electricity

In the picture there is also an example of static electricity: the balloon that is 'stuck' to the wall in the living room. How is it staying there? Can you think of other objects that use static electricity? (for example a feather duster)

Rubbing balloons

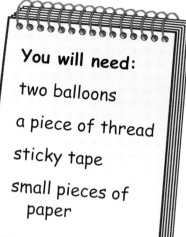

You will need:

two balloons

a piece of thread

sticky tape

small pieces of paper

 Blow up both balloons and tie the ends.

 Rub one balloon against your hair or your jumper.

 Try to get the balloon to stick to the wall or ceiling.

Does it work?

 Attach one end of the piece of thread to a desk using sticky tape.
Move the charged balloon above the thread.

What happens?

 Scatter some small bits of paper on the desk.
Move the charged balloon above them.

What happens?

 Rub both balloons together.

How do they affect each other?

 Draw and describe the results.

Rubbing balloons

Learning objective: to understand that you can charge things with static electricity, and that things with different charges are attracted to each other

Curriculum links

England/Wales:	Sc1 2a; Sc4 1a
Scotland:	SIS B; KUF A
Northern Ireland:	INC a

Investigation summary

Children rub a balloon against their hair or jumper to build up static electricity. They then try 'sticking' the balloon to the wall or ceiling. Next, they attach one end of a piece of thread to a desk using sticky tape, and pass the charged balloon above the thread. Then, they scatter some small bits of paper on the desk and move the charged balloon above them. Finally, they rub the balloon against another balloon and see how they affect each other.

Tips

This works best in the winter when it is cold and the air is dry. Hair should be dry when the balloon is rubbed against it. If you don't have balloons, you could use empty plastic bottles, polystyrene trays, plastic pens, plastic rulers or plastic combs.

Expected results

The balloon will be attracted to the ceiling or wall and stay there for quite a while. The thread can be made to sway in the air by passing the balloon back and forth above it. The pieces of paper will stick to the balloon. Two balloons rubbed together will repel each other.

Explanation

All matter consists of atoms. At the outside of the atom are the negatively charged electrons that revolve around the positively charged nucleus. Electrons are torn away from the strands of hair when the balloon is rubbed against them. The balloon acquires these extra electrons. The balloon is then charged with static electricity. The balloon clings to the ceiling because a field of positive charge builds up on the ceiling, so the negatively charged balloon is attracted to it. After a while, the extra electrons on the balloon will jump on to the ceiling, thereby neutralising both of them, causing the balloon to fall away. The charged balloon is attracted to the thread and the paper, which allows you to move them using the balloon. The two balloons repel each other because they are both negatively charged.

Everyday example

Sometimes you get a shock when you grip a door handle. This happens because your shoes have rubbed electrons off the carpet. Because air is a poor conductor, a discharge won't occur until you touch something conductive, such as the metal in a door handle.

Further ideas

You can also try using a charged balloon to pick up small grains of breakfast cereal, small balls of aluminium foil or a mixture of salt and pepper. The salt and pepper mixture is interesting because the pepper jumps up first.

Rubbing plastic bottles

 Rub the plastic bottle against your hair or jumper.

 Lay the can on the table.
Try to make it roll without touching it!

 Draw and describe what you did, and what happened.

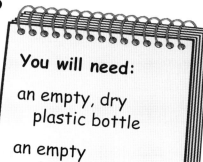

You will need:

an empty, dry plastic bottle

an empty aluminium can

Rubbing plastic bottles

Learning objective: to understand that statically charged objects can exert force on each other

Curriculum links

England/Wales: Sc1 2a; Sc4 1a

Scotland: SIS B

Northern Ireland: INC a

Everyday example

A feather duster cleans by attracting dust. When it is rubbed against the surface that it is dusting, it rapidly becomes charged. You will also see that the fibres of the duster repel each other. This is because they have the same charge.

Further ideas

You can also show that statically charged objects can rapidly discharge their charge. Sometimes you can even hear the electrical discharge. For this investigation you need a dark room and some aluminium foil. Go into the dark room and make a little mountain out of the foil. Charge a plastic bottle by rubbing it against your hair and move it closer and closer to the 'mountain'. In a very dark room you can both hear and see how the bottle discharges with a flash. This flash is the rapid flow of electrons.

We can compare this to what happens during a thunderstorm. A thundercloud is electrically charged. In most cases, the bottom of the cloud is negatively charged. This means that the ground directly under the cloud becomes positively charged. Discharge occurs when the cloud is close to the ground.

Investigation summary

Children rub an empty plastic bottle against their hair or a woollen or cotton jumper to charge it with static electricity. They then try to roll an empty aluminium can without touching it.

Tips

The cans that roll best are aluminium soft drink cans. Encourage the children to find out what happens when they rub the bottle against things other than hair, for example different types of paper or rubber.

Expected results

The can will be attracted to the plastic bottle. You can roll the can across the table by moving the bottle above the can.

Explanation

The plastic bottle rips electrons from the hair or jumper, and thus acquires extra electrons. When the bottle is moved towards the can, an area of positive charge is created and the can is attracted to the bottle. This is because a negative charge will always attract what is positively charged.

Can you light the bulb?

Can you think of a way to make the light *bulb* light up?

 Try different things to find out how to do it.

 Draw a big picture showing how you made it work.

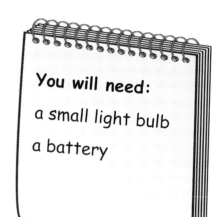

You will need:
a *small* light bulb
a battery

Can you light the bulb?

Learning objective: to understand that a light bulb will light up when it is part of a closed circuit

Curriculum links

England/Wales:	Sc4 1b, 1c
Scotland:	KUF C
Northern Ireland:	KPE a;
	KS2 KPE b

Investigation summary

Give each group of children a small light bulb (3.5 volts) and a 3LR12 battery (4.5 volts). Allow children to investigate for themselves ways to make the bulb light up.

The investigation may be carried out with standard cylindrical batteries but the children will need to be provided with at least one connecting wire.

Tips

Make sure that all the light bulbs work and that the batteries are reasonably new. Ask the children to draw large, clear pictures. If they draw the light bulbs as life size, the drawings will be too small.

Expected results

The following two connections work well:

Explanation

A battery has two poles – one positive and one negative. On the light bulb there are two areas that are 'contact seeking': the thread on the side and the knob on the bottom. If we connect the light bulb as shown in the above drawings we create a simple closed circuit through which electrons flow.

Further ideas

If you can get hold of one of those fluffy, battery-powered chicks that cheep when held in your hand (you can get them from markets or toy shops), you can demonstrate a circuit to the class. Using the contacts on the underside of the chick as positive and negative poles, you can build a 'circuit' using children holding hands to represent wires!

Home investigation

Static bag

 Blow up the plastic bag and tie a knot in the end.

 Rub the bag against your hair or a woollen jumper.

 Try to stick it to the wall or ceiling.

How long can you get it to stay there?

 Draw a picture to show what happened.

You will need:

a thin, plastic bag with no holes

Home investigation teacher notes

Static bag

Investigation summary

Children inflate a thin, plastic bag with no holes, and tie a knot in the end. They rub it against their hair or a woollen jumper. They investigate how long they can get the bag to cling to the wall or ceiling.

Tips

Investigations involving static electricity work best when the weather is cold and dry.

Expected results

The bag will stick to the wall and stay there a surprisingly long time – sometimes several hours.

Explanation

When the bag is rubbed against the hair or a natural fabric, electrons are torn away from the hair or fabric. The bag acquires a surplus of negative charges. Because negative charges attract positive charges, a field of the opposite charge is built up on the wall. After a while the electrons jump over to the wall. The bag will release when the difference in tension between the two surfaces is sufficiently small.

Further investigations

You will need: an old vinyl LP; a dry drinking glass; small bits of foil scrunched up into balls

Investigation

Rub the LP vigorously against your hair or a woollen jumper. Place the record on the top of the glass. Carefully sprinkle small balls of aluminium foil over the record. What do you see?

Expected results

The bits of foil will dance about in a very peculiar way!

Explanation

The static charge that is built up is not distributed evenly over the entire surface. The balls are affected by the charge at their particular landing site. In other words they are repelled by areas that share their charge and are attracted to areas with the opposite charge. The glass is there to insulate the record from the ground.

A short history of... electricity

Charged amber

Thales from Miletos (c. 625–547 BC) demonstrated that a piece of amber that had been rubbed against wool or fur generated a mysterious force that attracted feathers or straw. Methods of charging objects continued to develop and demonstrations of static electricity took on more and more spectacular proportions. One device consisted of a shovel wheel with pieces of amber attached to it that passed across the back of a live cat as it rotated!

Socks of different colours

When an English physicist took off one of the two pairs of silk socks he was wearing, he heard how they crackled. When he hung both pairs, one black and one white, on the clothes line, to his amazement he witnessed the following phenomenon: socks of the same colour repelled each other and socks of different colours attracted each other. His conclusion was that there must be two types of electricity.

The Voltaic pile

The knowledge that two different metals could generate electricity inspired Galvani's fellow countryman Alessandro Volta (1745–1827) to develop what became known as the Voltaic pile. This looked like a huge sandwich consisting of alternating layers of metal and salt-impregnated cloth. This primitive battery could maintain an electrical current for quite some time. The Voltaic pile was mass-produced and proved to be of great importance for future research.

Kites as lightning conductors

In 1752, Benjamin Franklin showed that the sparks generated in 'rubbing' experiments and lightning were the same type of phenomenon. You may have heard the story of how he flew a kite up into a thundercloud. The rope was wet and acted as a lightning conductor. At the end of the rope he tied a key. When his finger approached the key, a spark jumped over to it. This showed that thunder was an electric discharge.

Electric frogs' legs

One of the greatest challenges facing early scientists was finding a way to generate a continuous electrical current. One day, when the Italian scientist Luigi Galvani (1737–1798) was about to demonstrate a machine for generating electricity, he made a strange discovery. On a nearby table were several frogs' legs that he was going to use in another experiment. When the machine discharged, the legs started to jump! When he hung them on copper hooks and poked them with his iron scalpel, they started wriggling. He named this phenomenon 'animal electricity'.

Edison and the light bulb

Thomas Alva Edison (1847–1931) wanted to make 'electric light available to everyone'. The difficulty was finding a filament that wouldn't instantly burn up. His first step in the right direction was pumping all the air out of the glass container housing the filament. Suddenly the light worked for a whole 8 minutes! He still needed to find the right material. After having tried everything from monkey hair to palm fronds he finally tried a piece of carbonised sewing thread. On 21 October 1879, he turned on a light that worked for 40 hours. This was the world's first light bulb.